Praise for
Hope Unfolding

"Becky Thompson shares the truth of motherhood—the slob-
bery kisses and the heartwarming moments blended seamlessly
with the sleepless nights, tantrums, and never-ending piles of
laundry—while constantly pointing us back to the Father who
loves us beyond comprehension. In opening up a copy of *Hope
Unfolding,* readers are essentially invited to sit down over coffee
with a dear friend to talk about the real things in life. Becky is
our fellow mom friend who wrestles with the same questions
we do: 'Does what I'm doing matter?' 'Can I make it through
today?' 'Where is God in the dirty dishes?' In *Hope Unfolding*
we are offered space to ponder the truth of God's Word as
Becky offers a perspective of hope, gratitude, and grace in all
the moments of motherhood."

—LAUREN CASPER, founder of Laurencasper.com
and upcoming author with Thomas Nelson

"Becky Thompson's words are like a good cup of coffee: warm,
inviting, and the perfect soul refreshment in the everyday chaos
of motherhood. An encouraging, affirming, and uplifting read,
Hope Unfolding is the perfect gift of grace for every mom."

—KAYLA AIMEE, author of *Anchored: Finding
Hope in the Unexpected*

"Calling all moms in the trenches. Whether you are up to your eyeballs in diapers and dishes or dealing daily with homework and teens, this book is for you! In its pages you'll discover a respite from the rush and a dose of hope amidst the heartache that often accompanies motherhood. I wish I'd had this encouragement when my kids were small, and you can bet your sweet spit-up covered sweatshirt that all new moms I know will be gifted one from me at their baby showers. I can't recommend this grace-filled volume enough!"

> —KAREN EHMAN, *New York Times* best-selling
> author of *Keep It Shut* and *Hoodwinked,*
> Proverbs 31 Ministries speaker, wife and mother
> of three

"Becky's warm and vulnerable storytelling had me nodding yes throughout the pages of this book. *Hope Unfolding* will resonate with every momma who has ever played the comparison game, doubted herself, or just needed someone to say 'me too.'"

> —JESSICA N. TURNER, author of *The Fringe Hours:
> Making Time for You*

HOPE

Unfolding

BECKY THOMPSON

OF SCISSORTAIL SILK

WATERBROOK
PRESS

Hope Unfolding
Published by WaterBrook Press
12265 Oracle Boulevard, Suite 200
Colorado Springs, Colorado 80921

All Scripture quotations, unless otherwise indicated, are taken from the Holy Bible, New International Version®, NIV®. Copyright © 1973, 1978, 1984, 2011 by Biblica Inc.®. Used by permission. All rights reserved worldwide. Scripture quotations marked (KJV) are taken from the King James Version.

Trade Paperback ISBN 978-1-60142-812-7
eBook ISBN 978-1-60142-813-4

Published in the United States by WaterBrook Multnomah, an imprint of the Crown Publishing Group, a division of Penguin Random House LLC, New York.

WaterBrook® and its deer colophon are registered trademarks of Penguin Random House LLC.

Library of Congress Cataloging-in-Publication Data
Names: Thompson, Becky, (Rebecca F.) author.
Title: Hope unfolding : grace-filled truth for the momma's heart / Becky Thompson.
Description: First Edition. | Colorado Springs, Colorado : WaterBrook Press, 2016. | Includes bibliographical references.
Identifiers: LCCN 2015036784| ISBN 9781601428127 | ISBN 9781601428134 (electronic)
Subjects: LCSH: Mothers—Religious life.
Classification: LCC BV4529.18 .T466 2016 | DDC 248.8/431—dc23 LC record available at http://lccn.loc.gov/2015036784

Printed in the United States of America
2016—First Edition

10 9 8 7 6 5 4 3 2 1

Special Sales
Most WaterBrook Multnomah books are available at special quantity discounts when purchased in bulk by corporations, organizations, and special-interest groups. Custom imprinting or excerpting can also be done to fit special needs. For information, please e-mail SpecialMarkets@WaterBrookMultnomah.com or call 1-800-603-7051.

To my husband, Jared, and our children, Kolton, Kadence, Jaxton, and the ones who wait in Jesus's arms. Thank you for allowing me to share our stories. May they be used to ignite hope.

Contents

To You, Momma, Before We Begin. xi

Introduction 1
One More Thing to Hold

1. Diamonds in the Dirt 13
God Hasn't Forgotten About You

2. Ordinary Threads 29
God's Plans Are Perfect

3. A Fight for Joy 53
God Is Good Even When Life Isn't

4. Is It Just Me? 73
You're Not Alone

5. You Can't Do It All. 87
Let God Be Your Strength

6. Real Life Looks Lived In 105
   You Are Not Your Mess

7. Don't Run Her Race 125
   Have Grace for Who You Are

8. Outside the Box 145
   God Still Performs Miracles

9. The Father's Love for a Momma's Heart . . . 167
   God Loves You Just as You Are

10. The "Good Mom" Movement 183
    You Are Enough

Before We End 203
Acknowledgments 205
Notes 209

To You, Momma, Before We Begin

*H*i, friend. I am so glad that these words have found you. I don't know if they were gifted to you or if you picked them up while browsing your local bookstore. Perhaps you are reading black pixels across a white screen. However you have come across them, I think it is for a reason.

I imagine you reading these words while you steal a few minutes during nap time or eat your lunch at your desk. I imagine you reading them late at night when the house is quiet—or in the middle of the day when you grab five minutes to yourself while the kids are distracted with LEGOs or *Mickey Mouse.* I picture women just like you all over the world in waiting rooms, living rooms, and offices reading these words. We might not have met, but in my heart (and often in my writing), I call you friend.

We're a lot alike, you and I. We both have fears and worries, anxieties and stresses, hopes and dreams, situations and circumstances that we are going through at this very moment.

We are each in the middle of our own stories. But even though the details of our lives might be unique, I always look for where they intersect. I look for our common ground to re-mind us that we are not alone, and that the God of all creation is with us. In this, there is hope.

Take a deep breath with me. Would you?

Okay. Now here's the deal. In a minute, life will continue. The kids will need your attention, or you will have to return to work. There will be e-mails to respond to or customers that you must help. Your dishes will still need to be washed, the clothes folded, and the toys put away. You will still have meetings and appointments and people waiting for you. You will still have to decide what to do next. You will still have to face what is up ahead . . .

But just for a second, I was wondering if I could share my heart with you. I'm not asking you to do anything. Nope. Nothing.

I'm not asking you to give any more of yourself when you already feel spread thin. I'm not adding one more thing to your list of things to do. Today, friend, I want to give you permission to just *be.*

Yes. That's it.

I know there are some days when you feel overlooked and underappreciated. You feel overwhelmed by the demands you face and the responsibilities you shoulder. You worry if you're messing everything up, or if it's too late, or if it's all worth it.

There are times when you feel unloved and unseen—and moments when you feel like you're failing at all of it.

Friend, sometimes we just need hope. We need someone to look into our hearts and speak hope into every shadowed corner. And I'm so grateful to be the one who gets to do just that. And the one who can pray for you.

So, Lord?

I ask that You would speak to the heart of my new friend. I ask that You would walk through these pages and speak through these words and gently remind her heart that You are with her. I pray that through these stories You would bring hope and healing as she begins to trace Your workings and Your presence in her own life. And I ask that You would weave new life into every area that feels threadbare and worn thin. Thank You for hearing me, Lord. Thank You for responding just because You love me and You love the one reading these words. In Jesus's name I pray, amen.

These words are my stories and my heart for you, friend. May you know the truth of God's presence in your life as you discover that His love, His plans, and His promises for you are forever unfolding. And together we will find strength as we remember that in Him alone there is hope.

With love,

Becky

One More Thing to Hold

I have a white ceramic pitcher full of flowers that sits in my kitchen window. In the last year or so, I started collecting them (white pitchers, not windows). There is just something so clean and quaint and a little bit country about them. Also, I realized that most of the photos I pin to my "Dream Kitchen" board on Pinterest have a pitcher of flowers somewhere in the room.

If you've ever shopped for white pitchers, you know how hard they are to find. Well, they're hard to find until you find one, and then suddenly you find five, and the fact that you couldn't find any for so long makes you want to buy all five because Pinterest said you could put one in the window, and one on the kitchen table, and one on the bookshelf.

And so I bought all of them—hence the collection.

But my favorite is the small, simple pitcher that sits right in front of where I spend (what feels like) most of my day washing out sippy cups and scrubbing out bottles. I use it as a vase to hold my favorite flowers . . . and before you start picturing a well-arranged bouquet sitting in a well-organized kitchen, you need to know that by "favorite flowers" I mean cut flowers that I buy at the grocery store for $2.88.

Until last Mother's Day . . .

To Have and to Hold

My sweet husband, Jared, is always early for everything— unless he is planning for my birthday or Mother's Day or our anniversary. At this point, Jared's favorite line is "I'm sorry that I didn't get you a card. I just ran out of time."

I never say anything about it. I wouldn't say something to hurt him on purpose when I do know that he loves me and his time really is taken with all of his other obligations (like being a volunteer firefighter and our town mayor; serving at our church; or working his full-time, often-out-of-town job). If anyone could use the excuse that they just didn't have any time, it would be my Jared.

Hypothetically, if I were to say something, I might say, "Really? You ran out of time? Because it's not like Mother's Day was a surprise. As a matter of fact, you said the same thing last year, and that means you had exactly 365 days to buy a card or candy or a balloon. Don't tell me you ran out of time." I may or may not have thought of that comeback years ago. But I haven't said it because, really, I'm not that type of lady (unless I'm hungry or tired, in which case I cannot be held responsible for the things I say when I'm "hangry" or sleep deprived).

Anyway, two days before Mother's Day this past year, Jared arrived home early from work and brought with him a small plant covered in tiny pink flowers. "Here! These are for you! They are supposed to keep blooming!"

I wasn't expecting them. I wasn't really expecting anything at all. (*Hoping?* Yes. *Expecting?* No.)

As a mom of three little ones, ages five, four, and one, I am resigned to the fact that I will likely never get what I think I really want for Mother's Day. Don't get me wrong—cards and breakfast are great. Still, every year I fantasize that my husband is planning an elaborate celebration of my day-in, day-out dedication to our family and children. (A girl can dream, can't she?)

Each year, I imagine him arranging to gift me with a day off from all of my responsibilities. On this day off, everyone else would do all of the work that I usually do, then comment on how they didn't realize just how hard a mom's job really is. The day might include a trip to the salon or spa, after which I would return, feeling pampered and refreshed, to find a clean house with bathed children who have already been tucked into bed for the night. Glory.

I was mid-daydream, cucumbers over my eyes and tranquil

music playing softly in my ears . . . when my husband jolted me back to reality, holding out the flowers and spilling a little bit of potting soil onto the carpet.

"It's not just an arrangement. It's a plant! It keeps blooming!"

He was so proud of himself, and I really was grateful that he had thought of me. So I thanked him as Kolton, my five-year-old, shouted, "Happy Momma's Day!" His little sister, Kadence, sang it out about a beat behind him. They ran and hugged me, squishing their baby brother, Jaxton, whom I was holding on my lap.

And so I held all of them—my sweet babies and my new plant that, while beautiful, felt like one more thing that I had to take care of. I sat there in the middle of my living room, with full hands and a full heart, so thankful for the gift of children who make me Momma, while silently fighting back tears of stress. Sometimes the weight of adding one more thing to what we are required to hold makes us feel like we're going to drop everything.

Have you ever felt that way? Have you ever felt as if you cannot find a steady balance between being a wife and a momma? Have you ever felt overwhelmed by not only your motherhood but also by the reality of being a momma, while also trying to do everything else at the same time? Friend, you're not the only one. Sometimes, we don't even realize that we need hope until someone offers it. We don't even realize that we are desperate for someone to understand how we feel until we hear another woman say, "I have been there too."

I think that far too often we find hope in things that will fade away. We find hope in articles that tell us to get a better night's sleep or clean our kitchen before we go to bed or recite five proven prayers to find peace, balance, and a calm heart. But the truth is we need Jesus. We need an encounter with the only One who knows and understands and wants to meet us right where we are. And when we encounter that hope? When we reach out to the only One who can give us the authentic life-sustaining grace that we so desperately crave? We experience the difference between being buried in chaos and planted in His love.

Hope Unfolding

I am not a gardener. In spite of that, my husband and I have begun a garden in front of our house multiple times. Obviously, one only gets to experience the joy of beginning a garden multiple times if something happens to the previous garden. I will let you infer what you would like, but let's just say we kill all the plants.

This is not on purpose. We aren't purposeful plant killers. I read the labels. I buy plants that are hardy for our planting zone. (You should know that I feel fancy even knowing what *planting zone* means.) But despite my best efforts, until recently most of our plants didn't make it through the harsh Oklahoma winter. Which makes me think of *Little House on the Prairie* . . . and covered wagons and salt-cured pork. In case you haven't been to Oklahoma in a while (or ever), I feel like I should mention that we have come a long way. But back to the plants.

I kill all of them. Every time.

So, when Jared handed me that sweet little plant with the tiny pink blooms on Mother's Day, I felt like I should apologize to it. It had surely lived a healthy and happy plant life before it arrived at my house. It wasn't the plant's fault that it had been gifted to me.

But instead of writing its eulogy, I decided to do my best to take care of it. I moved it from one window to the next, setting it in different sunny places around my house. Once I even took it out onto the back porch for some morning light. I watered it. I cared for it. But before long, despite all of my best efforts, the tiny pink flowers withered and fell off, one after the other, until there were no blooms left.

I wondered what I had done wrong. It felt like proof of my failure, and for some reason—probably because it was a

Mother's Day gift—I related the health of this small plant to my success as a momma.

The baby had skipped his morning nap, my older two kids were fighting, the house was in a general state of chaos, and I couldn't even keep this small plant alive for two weeks. I needed a win. That's when I decided to let my plant live the last of its days in my favorite pitcher in my window.

The pitcher had been empty for a while. Even though I did my best to always have flowers of some kind in it, it had sat empty in my window for over a month.

I pulled the makeshift vase off the window ledge and ran some hot water inside, swishing it around and then pouring the dirty water into the kitchen sink. I wiped down its warm ceramic sides and dried off the last of the droplets. I reached over and gently rocked the small plant from its container, being careful not to break the delicate stem as bits of dirt fell, leaving the roots exposed. I scooped up some of the soil left in the pot, using my hand as a shovel. I poured it into the pitcher and then carefully lowered the plant in on top of it, packing dirt around the base.

It's still green, so maybe it still has a shot, I thought. *Maybe it's not hopeless after all.*

Honestly, each morning, I was surprised when I would go into the kitchen to start breakfast and find that the plant was still alive. Life has a way of surprising us like that sometimes, doesn't it? So as long as the plant wasn't giving up, I decided that I wasn't either. I watered it every few days and enjoyed having something in the pitcher again. And the plant kept living. One day after another, with just a little bit of water and a little bit of sunlight, the plant just kept living, and eventually tiny pink blooms covered it again.

I guess that is the difference between cut flowers and a flower that has been planted in good soil and prepared for growth. A bouquet in a vase might look pretty, but it doesn't have what it takes to keep growing. And the same is true for us.

Friend, I know how overwhelmed your heart sometimes feels, and I know how down-to-the-bone tired—yes, completely exhausted—you are most days. I know what it feels like to spend hour after hour holding or rocking or feeding a fussy baby, a sick baby, or a baby who just refuses to close his precious little eyes. I know how small hands that shake us in the night to tell us about a bad dream or cries that send us running into door frames and across LEGO minefields can make for a long day.

I know how restless nights can make today feel like an extension of yesterday. And yesterday an extension of the day before. And how all of your days seem to run together. I know what it feels like to be standing in a place where tomorrow looks like more of the same, with no end in sight.

I get it. Momma, I totally get it.

Maybe you woke up ready for today to be different. Happy

attitudes, extra patience, and NO YELLING! And maybe by 8:15 a.m. you realized that it was going to be another day full of cranky babies, demanding toddlers, and guilt from losing your temper when you could have just taken a deep breath and calmly repeated your request to your five-year-old . . . for the hundredth time.

Maybe breakfast, or lunch or dinner, is still out on the counter, and you can't stop to clean it up because you have to find another pair of Buzz Lightyear undies since all of those online articles on how to potty train your kid in thirty-six hours were a bunch of bunk.

Maybe you're out of diapers, and the milk has gone bad, and the bill you paid a week ago got lost in the mail. Maybe you're about to run to the grocery store with hungry kids, while wearing a sweatshirt over last night's pajamas.

Maybe you're on your third ear infection this month, or it feels like you have visited the doctor's office so often that you should have your own reserved parking spot. Maybe everything that could go wrong has gone wrong and nothing seems fixable; you don't know how you'll make it, but you keep going because there are no other options and if you come undone then everything and everyone else will come unraveled with you.

Sweet friend, I hear you. Sometimes I want to scream when I read words that tell me to cherish these moments. These moments of pure exhaustion when I am hanging on by a thread. When I don't remember the last time I had a proper meal or felt like I wasn't in charge of *everything*. When my heart wasn't torn by the guilt of craving a moment for myself, while knowing that I should appreciate the gift of having a family to love.

Because we already know it's true. We know that one day we will look around and miss all of this madness. But today— in the middle of it—we don't need to add guilt to our exhaustion, and we certainly don't want to have to add "find joy" to our to-do list.

We just need hope (and maybe a long, uninterrupted nap).

We need to know that somewhere someone else feels the same way that we do. We need to believe that we aren't alone. And beyond having hope that tomorrow could be different, we need to know that there is purpose in where we are standing today.

Friend, there is only one way that we are going to have the strength to keep going. There is only one way that we are going to have all that it takes to love our families with the love that they deserve, the love we so desperately want to give them. We must become rooted in the Truth of who God is calling us to be by hearing and believing the Truth of who He says that we already are.

So, for the next few chapters, I want to water your heart

with the hope of God's love and Truth. I want to remind you that you're not alone. As I share stories from my own life, and point to the places where hope began to grow unexpectedly for me, I want you to recognize the areas where new life is possible for you. And as I share some of the things that God has spoken to my heart, I want you to begin to listen to what He is saying to yours. Friend, in the pages ahead, we will chat about the things that weigh heaviest on our mommy hearts. Some of those areas don't get spoken of often. Some of those places are shadowed and hidden. But as we shine light on those areas, we will begin to see the promise of the new growth. We will see that our stories are still being written.

If I could, I would ask you over to my house. While the kids ran and played, you and I would sit and chat. We would dialogue back and forth; we would dream and hope together. But because that's not possible (well, not today anyway), at the end of each chapter, we will have a chance to reflect together. There are a few questions that might put into words what your heart has been asking, and some space to journal your responses. My hope is that you would use this space to clear your heart of any heavy concerns and to give life to some of your forgotten dreams. And as we spill out our stories together, we will pray and ask the Lord to continue the good work that He has begun in both of us.[1] I am so grateful for the chance to spend a few minutes with you, and I am even more honored that you would give me the chance to remind you of God's goodness.

You and I are going to be okay, friend, because together we are going to plant ourselves in grace and let the Lord wash over us with His love as we experience the miracle of tiny pink flowers blossoming . . . and hope unfolding.

1

Diamonds in the Dirt

GOD HASN'T FORGOTTEN ABOUT YOU

wo years ago, and seven years into our marriage, I stood over our mudroom sink with my husband's wedding ring and a toothbrush in my hand. I began to scrub the Oklahoma red dirt from around the small diamonds. The loose sand and clay pooled in the sink, then slowly slipped down the drain. I tried to imagine the last of my expectations washing away as well.

I turned the ring over in my hand and remembered the day that the jewelry store lights first reflected off it. When we were choosing the wedding band, I had tried to imagine it on my husband's finger as he held the microphone at the front of the church. It was exactly what I imagined a pastor would wear. Not just a plain band, but not too much sparkle either. We weren't aiming for a flashy 1990s televangelist look; we were just trying to communicate that the handsome young pastor was unmistakably married. The white gold band with three diagonal lines of diamonds announced it perfectly.

I scrubbed some more and held it up to see if I had removed all of the clay. The ring didn't sparkle like it used to. It was scuffed and dulled, and no matter how much I polished, I couldn't remove all of the life that had settled into the cracks.

Let's be honest. The blistering Oklahoma sun is hardly comparable to stage lights. The ditches where my husband, a welder, spends his days laying natural gas pipelines aren't exactly the same as church platforms. As I held that small circle in my hand, the perfect symbol of our marriage and life together, I couldn't help but think that we had chosen a ring for a different life. Because what I expected isn't anything at all like the way it turned out.

Deep down, I was afraid that all of the people who questioned our quick engagement and young vows were right. I was afraid that all of the people who said that we hadn't had a chance to grow up before we committed our lives to each other weren't wrong after all. I had done my best to ignore them when Jared and I were married when I was just nineteen. I had done my best to pull up those sprouting seeds of doubt that said we would never make it. But sometimes we push things down when we should be pulling them up, and we don't realize the difference until they begin to grow.

Has anyone ever doubted a major decision that you have made? Have you ever stood in the place where the opinions of others have made even your most confident choices seem questionable? Maybe it was something simple. Maybe you were trying to decide if you should continue to try to breastfeed or switch to formula. Or maybe it was something bigger. Perhaps you were deciding if you would stay at home or go back to work. I know it can be hard to move forward when we feel like others don't support us or our choices. How do we remain confident in our decisions when it seems as if we will be moving forward alone? The truth is, once that seed of doubt has been planted, it doesn't take much for it to begin to take root. That's exactly what I began to experience as my life began to unfold.

I had always wanted to be a momma. I wanted a house full of babies and a man who loved Jesus and his family. I wanted to be a wife. But as I stood in the middle of all of my dreams coming true, I couldn't help but feel like maybe I had missed something somewhere. There were still all of these other things that I desired—hopes, dreams, plans. But my to-do list on my calendar didn't line up with the passions in my heart. I was overwhelmed trying to balance life as wife and a mother. I was needed by everyone, and yet I felt unseen in the story of my own life.

What did I still want to do? Who did I want to be when I grew up? Was this really how it all turned out in the end? It was like a steady beat on the door of my heart—a call to something bigger than myself—a reminder that there was a time when not only did I get to sleep, but I dreamt too.

I just had to decide that the passions and plans deep inside of me were still worth remembering. And friend, the things that are in your heart should not be forgotten either. Jesus places desires in our hearts for a reason. But to recognize this, and explain how He worked it all out in His timing, I have to go all the way back to the beginning. Back to the day that a cookie changed everything.

The Day That Determined My Future

Some love stories start in a college classroom, or at a crowded holiday party, or on a blind date arranged by mutual friends. The story of Jared and me started with some new clothes and a cookie.

I had just finished my first two semesters of college in Tulsa, Oklahoma, and I was staying at my parents' house in Norman for the summer. I decided to fill my free time with an easy job at a nearby mall. (Okay, I'll be honest. I did it for the employee discount I would get on the clothes.)

I had worked retail in high school. Back then, there were many times when girls came in asking for a job and were hired on the spot. So I decided that I would try that approach. It worked, and I was offered a job at one of my favorite shops. But as I left the store and headed toward the parking lot, a small voice in my heart said, *"Keep walking."* It wasn't just some thought I had. It was a voice. It was clear, and it was one I had heard many times earlier in my life. So I listened. Besides, who was I to argue with a voice that tells me to spend a little more time at the mall?

Following my heart, I came around a corner just as a young woman placed a Now Hiring sign on the counter of a small clothing kiosk. It was too much of a coincidence not to approach her.

"You are hiring?" I asked, pointing to the sign.

The woman replied with a thick Russian accent. "Yesss. Vhhaaat is your experience?"

I instantly felt as though she would be hard to please, but I gave it my best shot. "Um. I worked in a clothing store during high school, and I am very reliable, and I'm very responsible." I ended with an exaggerated smile.

She glared at me, thought for a moment, and then became the second person to offer me a job in that hour. Also, she might not have actually been glaring. I never could tell if she was always slightly agitated, or if that was just her beautiful stern face. Either way, I was told to come back the next day for training. I agreed. And I quickly resigned from the other store.

It wasn't a fast-paced job. I sat on a stool in the middle of the mall, waiting for people to walk by and buy black flowy gaucho pants and sequin-covered elastic belts that were shipped in from Los Angeles. And while we are discussing this, I feel like I should say, "Dear Lord, thank You that one day we all woke up and decided that neither of those clothing items was a good idea. Amen." (If you happen to be reading this when flowy gaucho pants and sequined-covered belts are totally in style again, then good for you. Let the record show, at one point back in 2005, I was a trendsetter. You're welcome, future gaucho wearer.)

About halfway through my first day on the job, I quickly realized that I was going to need a little help with my kiosk when it came to taking breaks. (It's not like those freestanding shops have potties somewhere.) So I asked the guy working at the shoe store right next to the cart if he would watch my shop while I ran to the restroom. Of course, I should add here that I needed an excuse to talk to him, because, y'all, he was *handsome*. I tried to be cute while I asked him to watch my cart, but that's hard to pull off when you have to pee.

"Hey," I said, sounding over-the-top flirty.

"Hey," he replied, overly chill and laid back.

"Do you think you could watch my cart while I . . . take a break for a second?" I asked, batting eyelashes but fooling no one.

"Sure."

He was clearly interested in me. So, I bought him a cookie to say thank you. Six months later, he bought me a ring.

THAT TIME I WAS SO WRONG

I really had no intention of falling for Jared. I was home just for the summer, and my plan was to return to school in the fall and find a nice guy who would one day become a pastor. At the time, I fully believed that if you wanted to devote your entire life to changing the world with the love of God, and you also wanted to be married, then you should find a man with a similar calling. While this is obviously not always necessary, this is what eighteen-year-old me believed. I mean, some girls grow up dreaming of what they want to be, and I grew up dreaming of what God might use me to do to advance His kingdom. I had encountered God at a very young age, and I wanted to see other people's lives transformed by an encounter with Jesus as well. More than anything else, I wanted to be that person who led others to Him.

Making plans for the future, I decided that I wanted a husband who would be my partner in ministry as well as life. (Side note: I have learned since then that when it comes to future planning, it's always best to leave it up to the One who has already been there.)

Jared was on his own path. He was a country boy who was

working toward becoming a police officer. Clearly (well, at least it was clear to me), we could be friends but nothing more. I made this known to him from the beginning. I guess it might be a little awkward to admit, but I remember telling him, "Someday I am going to be a pastor's wife." He was not going to be a pastor, so I might as well have said, "Look. You are super handsome. As a matter of fact, when we talk, I'm usually distracted by your good looks, but this [I gesture toward him and back toward me] isn't going anywhere." It is funny how sometimes we nearly miss God's perfect plan because we are so busy coming up with our own—even when we have the best intentions at heart.

Jared and I spent a lot of time together in those short summer months. It wasn't anything serious, but there was something about Jared that seemed . . . significant. I couldn't quite figure out what pulled my heart to his, but to speed this story up a bit, our friendship grew into love, and six months after that voice in the mall told me to keep walking, the same voice whispered, *"Say yes when he asks."*

Naturally, this could only mean one thing. If I was going to marry a pastor someday, and Jared was the guy for me, then Jared wasn't going to become a police officer. Obviously, God was going to do some redirecting in Jared's life, and he would become a pastor at the end of the story. Right? I had it all figured out. We would dedicate our entire lives to sharing the gospel. We would be teachers of the Word, lovers of the brokenhearted, and revivalists for the kingdom of God! At least, that was my plan. You can imagine my confusion when, three years into our marriage, Jared suggested that we move with our six-month-old son to his small hometown in the middle of NW Oklahoma to work for his family's natural gas pipeline construction business.

Surely, he couldn't be serious. Surely, one of us had misheard the Lord . . . and surely it wasn't me.

Have there been any plot twists in your story that you didn't see coming? A surprise phone call from your husband to announce a job transfer, or a positive pregnancy test that you just didn't expect? Have you found yourself working when you planned on staying home with your babies, or staying at home when you had a career path mapped out? What did you do? How did you respond? Probably better than I did when I realized that things weren't going to be much like I had imagined. It is hard to have grace for the way things are when our lives aren't much like what we had imagined they would be.

There's nothing wrong with saying, "I'm not sure what I was hoping for, but I am sure that this is not it." But what do we do then? How do we reconcile our expectations with our realities? What do we do when nothing in life feels much like what we thought it would? And how do we find hope when it feels like nothing could possibly ever change?

You know, I suppose the day before everything changes

feels like just another ordinary day. It is not until we look back that we realize something significant was about to happen, and we didn't even see it coming. That's where my story really begins. In the middle of my ordinary day, in the middle of NW Oklahoma.

Back Road Revival

Yes. It's true. We ended up in a very small town in NW Oklahoma where Jared works for his family's company. I like to joke that NW isn't just the abbreviation for *northwest,* but more accurately stands for "No Where." I have come to love this place and love the people here, but I have to be honest. The first time that Jared brought me to his parents' house, I was secretly concerned that he was taking me to the middle of nowhere to drop me off for good. I kept thinking, as he drove farther and farther away from civilization, *How well do I really know this guy? Will anyone ever find me out here? Are we the first people to ever drive down this back road?*

Seriously. If you want to find my house, drive until you say to yourself, *Where are we?* And then keep going fifteen more minutes. We're the second house on the left. Friend, I have wheat fields for neighbors, more unwelcome critters than I care to admit, and the nearest Walmart or Starbucks is forty minutes away. Yes, *forty.*

This was never supposed to be my story.

When we moved into my husband's old basement bedroom in his parents' house with our six-month-old baby—while we decided where we were going to live long-term—I remember thinking, *Well, if there was any hope left that my life would turn out even a little like I had imagined, it is gone.* Each step seemed to take me further away from everything I had planned, and if the demands of being a new mom and a young wife were not enough, I began to feel lost in my own life.

Remember, I was going to change the world with the love of God. I was going to reach the nations with the transforming Truth of Jesus Christ! How was I supposed to do that from my tiny town, while living in my in-laws' basement? How could I possibly make a difference as a stay-at-home momma consumed with the day-to-day tasks of taking care of my baby, my house (well, my corner of my in-laws' house), and my husband (who clearly was not interested in becoming a pastor)? And where on earth was God in all of this?

Friend, maybe there are moments when you have felt the same way. You had plans that have been set aside. You had dreams that now seem more like shadows. And like me, all of your sparkly expectations have turned out a little muddier than you imagined. But this moment, right where you are, is no surprise to God. He didn't wake up this morning and say, "Wow! How'd we end up here?" then shrug His shoulders and shuffle off to get some coffee (even though there are days that feel as if that is His general attitude). He has been with you every step of the way. Even the ones that didn't make any sense. Sometimes, we just have to be willing to admit that even if it doesn't look anything like we thought it would, God knew exactly where we would end up all along . . . even if it seems like we have been forgotten in the middle of nowhere. And you and I are not the first to feel this way.

From the Beginning

Eve was the first woman that God made. She and her husband, Adam, were placed in a garden, perfectly cared for by God, and were given one command: "Don't eat the fruit from this one particular tree." That seems simple enough. Just don't eat this fruit. But she eats the fruit, and disobeys God, and God says basically, "Okay, well, you disobeyed, and now you cannot stay in the garden with Me anymore." (But we don't realize why God did this until later in the story.)

See, God had a plan. Because He always has a plan. He wasn't surprised by Eve's choices. He wasn't surprised by Adam and Eve's relocation to a new neighborhood outside of the Garden of Eden. God knew that He would send His Son, Jesus, to die as the sacrificial Lamb to redeem humanity and draw them back to Himself. Scripture says that Jesus's sacrifice was prepared long before Adam and Eve ever took those fateful bites. The book of Revelation confirms this.

But until then, God also knew that Adam and Eve couldn't stay in the garden. Because there was also this other tree in the garden called the tree of life, and as long as Adam and Eve continued to eat from it, they would continue to have eternal life. So, listen to this: God loved Adam and Eve so much that once they disobeyed Him and separated themselves from Him, He couldn't let them stay in the garden and eat from the tree of life because then they would live forever separated from Him. He loved them too much to allow them to live outside of His presence forever. So He made it so they couldn't get to the tree of life and He made sure that He would be able to save all of humanity through Jesus later on.

But I bet at that time Adam and Eve didn't understand that part of their story. From their perspective, there was no way to comprehend what God had in store. You know, sometimes we have to be willing to trust God to lead us down the roads that don't make any sense if we want to continue to walk in His perfect plan. We have to trust that He doesn't just have our best interests at heart but the interests of those that we love as well.

Whatever you are trusting Him with, whatever steps you are taking or see ahead that you need to take, I want you to look at them as the safest route to your future. Because even when we don't understand them, we can trust that God is ordering them purposefully forward. And I have learned it is often just when we think we are truly lost that we realize even the back roads can take us exactly where we were supposed to be all along.

And that is exactly what I did. One step after the other, I followed the Lord as He led me where I least expected to go — right where I wanted to be all along. It just happened to take a little longer to recognize it once I arrived.

Let's Talk

Does it ever feel as if God has forgotten about you and your dreams? Do you ever wonder why God would place all of these dreams in your heart, only to forget you now? It can be easy to feel as though there is no way for things to change. It can be easy to believe that life will always be just like it is right now, but God isn't done writing your story. What if I reminded you that even the most unspectacular moments are all steps on the path down which God is calling your heart? What would it mean if you truly believed that you haven't missed God's plan? That He hasn't forgotten about you? That He is still working it all out for your good? Think back to what you dreamt of doing when you were younger. How would you live if you believed that anything was still possible?

_____

_____

_____

❧ Let's Pray

Lord, thank You for the dreams that You have placed in our hearts. Thank You for the desires that burn (even dimly) deep within us. Sometimes the obligations that we carry as wives and moms seem to suffocate the flame of hope within us. We feel overwhelmed by the demands of our days and the reality that there doesn't seem to be a break in sight. God, this doesn't leave much room for dreaming. This doesn't leave much space for considering what we would like to do for us when we are so consumed with taking care of everyone else. So, Lord, I ask that You would stir up our hearts for the things that You've called us to do. Fan the flame of hope as we search Your heart and find purpose in Your presence. Help us to cling to the truth that You have not forgotten about us, and we have not missed Your plans for us. In Jesus's name we pray, amen.

❧ Let's Hope (Say This with Me!)

God isn't done with me yet! He has a plan for me. I will choose to trust Him.

2

Ordinary Threads

GOD'S PLANS ARE PERFECT

*I*t was a couple summers ago when I opened my closet to get out the warm weather clothes and quickly realized that I had none. We had moved from my in-laws' basement into a house that we had built on the edge of the small town where we now live. Kolton was three, Kadence was two—and I was still wearing my maternity shorts with the giant elastic belly, even though Jaxton wasn't even a twinkle in my husband's eye. (Am I the only one who thinks that phrase is creepy?)

Anyway, it was summer, and my wardrobe choices were maternity shorts from two years earlier or prepregnancy shorts from four years earlier, but neither felt like a good idea. There are a few things that should change after you have children, and I personally believe that the length of a woman's inseam is one of them (but I judge not).

So one day, after getting dressed in a T-shirt and my maternity shorts, I caught a reflection of myself in the mirror, and I immediately decided to go shopping. And then I quickly changed my mind. Because let's be real. Getting myself and my two very young children dressed to go out into public wasn't a simple task. There was potty prep, packing the diaper bag—including but not limited to extra clothes, underwear, toenail clippers (because you never knew when someone was going to have a hangnail meltdown), sippy cups, pacifiers, bottles, and snacks—and that was what it took to simply get out the door. We don't need to go into detail about the car seats and strollers, the complaining and whining, and the lollygagging and desperate potty breaks once we actually arrive. Oh, and while I'm taking care of all of that, I am supposed to find clothes, try them on, and make clear-headed, logical purchases without just throwing things on the counter and saying, "Surely there is something decent in here that fits."

No. Just . . . no. I decided I would rather wear my awesome elastic-waisted maternity shorts for another summer before I took two toddlers shopping with me.

Back when I worked at the mall, I enjoyed finding just the right pieces to go together. As a matter of fact, while I waited for shoppers to stroll by my kiosk, I busied myself by doodling notebooks full of different looks for the clothing that I had in my closet. I'd like to think of myself as the original Pinterest fashion board.

When my kids came along, style didn't matter anymore. There were no sketches of which shoes to wear with which top or which earrings paired best with each blouse. Clean mattered, but even that wasn't always an option for this mommy. In between getting my toddler up and making a bottle for the baby, I usually grabbed the nearest, least spit-up-on thing that didn't require a hanger or an iron, then threw it on.

That day, when I looked in the mirror, I suddenly realized how moms get *style stuck*. You know what I'm talking about. They wear the same blue eye shadow and feathered bangs twenty years after it stopped being fashionable, because it was the last thing they knew to do before they stopped having the time to care. I wasn't going to let that happen to me. I decided that I *wanted* to care. I decided that I *wanted* to be crazy and, I dunno, brush my hair and put on a shirt that required some thought. Not because it was particularly important, or even because it made me feel important. I guess I just missed feeling like I had invested in myself.

I had seen a mom like me in the grocery store years before . . . the type of mom I swore that I would never become. Do you remember seeing those other moms back before you had kids and thinking, *That will NEVER be me. I would die before I wore an oatmeal-crusted T-shirt with pants like that in public. At least, I hope that's oatmeal. Doesn't she care about herself? Doesn't she care about the example she is setting for her children?* HA! In reality, when we meet that mommy in the mirror just a few years later, we think, *I was so wrong—so very wrong. She wasn't lazy. She was just the opposite. She just didn't have a minute for herself!* The things we said we would never do. Am I right? But it was the summer of the two-year-old maternity shorts when I realized that maybe I needed to take a minute and decide that I was worth my own attention again.

This was all in the back of my mind while I was browsing Facebook one afternoon during naptime. (Side note—Naptime is good for three things: 1. napping while your child naps, 2. cleaning up or getting a start on dinner, and 3. doing anything mindless that requires no questions answered or juice boxes opened. Can we agree that option two is nobody's favorite? And that option three wins nine times out of ten?)

Anyway, while on Facebook, I noticed that a friend of mine "liked" an online clothing boutique called Hazel & Olive, so I clicked on the link to check it out myself. I found that they had reasonable prices, free shipping, and free returns . . . and the clothes were cute! Clicking a few buttons from my couch seemed so much easier than dragging my crew to the mall. So I bought a few things and waited for them to come in the mail. When they did, I added them to the small section of my closet that I like to call "If I ever need an outfit that isn't spit-, snot-, or spill-proof." It doesn't need to be said that this portion of my closet is rarely visited. I guess I had forgotten why I wore the maternity shorts and T-shirts in the first place. *Hello? Because they are practical.* But I had purchased something for me, and I was going to do my very best to visit that part of my closet more frequently (meaning in about five to seven years, give or take a few).

A few weeks later, I noticed the same boutique was holding an online giveaway in an attempt to gain new Facebook followers. The rules were simple: "Upload a photo of yourself wearing one of our items. The photo with the most 'likes' wins $100 worth of free clothes." And I probably don't need to remind you that I have strong feelings about free/discounted clothes.

So, I did what any other momma in my position would do. I took off my pajama pants and T-shirt, put on my new outfit (that still had the tags attached), and went to take a photo of myself in my bathroom mirror. I felt a little ridiculous, honestly. My kids were banging on the bathroom door shouting, "Moooooommmma!"

And my response was, of course, "Just a second. Mommy is taking a selfie!"

I uploaded the photo to the boutique's Facebook page competition, and then I became the most annoying person on Facebook. I contacted everyone I had ever known and begged them to click on my picture and "like" it. I'm not joking. Some of the people that I messaged I hadn't talked to in years. I wrote something to the effect of, "Hey, hope your life turned out okay. Can you do me a favor and 'like' this picture?" Looking back, I feel a little embarrassed, but anything for free clothes, I guess. So all that work, and you're guessing that I won, right? Nope. But a few weeks later, I got something even better. The owner of the boutique sent me an e-mail.

Get this. She wanted to know if I was a fashion blogger. I kind of felt like I was being pranked. Me? A fashion blogger? I had to laugh considering the reality of my life. So I replied,

Dear boutique owner,

NO. Surprisingly, I'm not a fashion blogger. I had to take off my nasty mommy stuff to take a picture for your contest, and then I put the mommy clothes right back on so I wouldn't ruin them when I walked out of my bathroom and into my real life. While I enjoy the idea that someday I might be fashionable again, the reality is that I will likely get to wear that shirt I bought from you once in the next 365 days. I am more like a walking advertisement for *What Not to Wear.*

Yours truly,

Maternity shorts and spit up

Actually, I think my official response said something more like, "No."

You can imagine how surprised I was when a few days later she replied, "Oh, that's too bad. Because if you were a fashion blogger, I would pay you to advertise for me, and I would send you free clothes to feature each month."

Wait a second. Did she say "free clothes"?

Suddenly, I "remembered."

"Oh? Did I say that I was *not* a fashion blogger? Because what I really meant to say was that I am just starting a fashion blog, and I would love for you to be a sponsor. Where do I sign?"

Free clothes!

I set up a blog, picked out a few items, and uploaded my very first fashion post.

And that's when God spoke again, as I was driving down Highway 412 in NW Oklahoma. God talks to me a lot while I'm driving. It must be the serenity of my minivan full of Disney movies playing on the DVD player and screaming/hungry/thirsty/bored kids. But somehow, over all of that ruckus, I heard the Lord's words as plainly as you're reading mine, *"Becky. I'm going to give you an audience, and you will be responsible for them."*

My heart leapt! I knew that voice well. And so I agreed. "Yes, Lord. If You are giving me an audience, and You want me to be responsible for them, then I will make sure that they are the best-dressed audience, Jesus." I didn't realize what He was actually saying at the time. I had no idea that fashion would just be the doorway that would lead to a much bigger adventure. I had no idea that I was living some of my last ordinary days, because He was about to show me that all of those dreams He had placed in my heart were not hopeless after all.

I have spent a lot of my life trying to figure out what the next step looks like before it happens. I like to see the big picture. Not that I'm super organized or want to be fully prepared for what's coming up ahead. I guess it is just more that I want to be in the loop. Who really likes feeling left out—especially where her own life is concerned? Do you ever do this? Do you ever think about where you are and wonder what is just beyond your line of sight? *When will we have another baby? Where will my husband or I be professionally in the next year? Should we stay here or move to a better school district?*

I suppose this is what spurred so many days and nights where I would plead with God to show me what things would look like when the picture was finished. In college it was, *Who will I marry?* Once I married Jared, it was, *Where do we go from here?* And once my kids came along, I wondered, *Can this really be it? Is this what being a mom feels like all the time? Or is there something just over the horizon that will change everything?*

I would pray and ask the Lord for direction, all the while peering ahead into the dimly lit future, straining my eyes to see if there was something coming that I could recognize. But I never could. I never could see past the hand that the Lord was silently extending to me, simply asking me to trust Him a little bit further.

The more I think about it, the more I realize why He didn't tell me how things would turn out in the end. It's because I couldn't have understood from where I was. It is because He knows me, and He knows that if I had seen this moment coming—if I had seen the wheat fields and the dirt roads and the middle of nowhere as a part of the story—I wouldn't have trusted His plan. I might have even tried to change it. I'm good at that. I like to try things on and see how they feel and if they're a good fit. But friend, life isn't an outfit that we can just put on or take off. Life is like a garment that has been intricately woven from carefully chosen thread, each moment and each event coloring the design and shaping the finished work.

Our lives are made up of a million perfectly placed choices by the One who already knows how it turns out in the end. The beautiful truth is that the Master's hands can take ordinary threads and weave them into something extravagant.

It was exactly what He is doing with all of my moments. And, friend, it is exactly what He is doing with all of your moments too. He's busy spinning threads.

JESUS IS MY FRIEND

Being a fashion blogger was fun. I enjoyed creating outfits again. It reminded me a little of the summer that I met Jared. In the middle of all of my mommy duties, I had a reason to fix my hair and put on makeup and find an outfit that was selected for reasons other than being handy and cleanish. But the more that I began to post pictures and write about clothes, the more my heart (and my husband) reminded me that there were things I wanted—no, *needed*—to say. Things that wouldn't just help the other mommas and women who read my words feel good about the clothes they wore, but would help them know that the woman who wore the clothes was good too. I started to look for the real stories worth sharing in my life, but I didn't have to look very far. God was already setting the next scene. I just had to decide if I was going to trust Him when He asked me to step outside my comfort zone.

Have you ever told someone that Jesus loves them? I mean, beyond speaking to your children or your spouse or people that you know well. Have you ever walked up to a stranger and just said, "Jesus loves you," or gone out of your way to make this truth a reality to a stranger? I had not, as of two years ago. Nope. Never. I was the girl who wanted to dedicate her life to showing the world the love of Jesus, and yet on my own, I had never gone out of my way to share the news with a single stranger. It wasn't that I said no when Jesus asked me to—I just hadn't been listening for opportunities to say yes. That all changed one day at lunchtime.

It was 2013, the same summer that I began the fashion blog. On special days that summer (also known as the days that I didn't feel like making lunch), I would take the kids to get chicken salad sandwiches at our local café, and we would have a picnic at our house. This was one of those days. We were going to grab food to take home to eat.

Except, it wasn't going to be lunch as usual. I mean, that's how it started, but that's definitely not how it ended.

I stood there at the counter, trying to place our order, while simultaneously attempting to keep my sweet two-year-old girl's fingers out of a giant Mason jar containing Rice Krispies treats. I looked down to ask my son if he wanted soup to go with our sandwich, and I realized that he was not standing next to his sister. He was standing very close to a man who was eating his lunch at a table nearby. Not only was he standing very close to this man, he was smiling and waving at the man. Honestly, it was a little awkward.

This guy didn't notice Kolton right away, but when he turned, I think he was a little startled. The guy looked at me and nodded, obviously trying to see if there was some connection between this kid who was acting like he knew him and the parent who obviously didn't. I shrugged my shoulders and turned around to pay. *Sorry, guy,* I thought. *I don't know why my kid is doing that. I think it is a little weird too, truthfully.* My son continued to stand there a minute longer just smiling at this guy, my daughter begged me for a cookie, and I was just trying to get the food and get back to our car. (I always wished that place had a drive-through.)

A few seconds later, my son ran back over to me and said, "Mommy, I waved at that man and smiled. He is a nice man. He waved at me . . . Does he know JEEEESUS?!"

Gulp. He had announced this question in the middle of a busy small-town café at lunch. Plenty of folks crammed into the little room, and I'm looking around, wondering how to respond.

"I don't know, baby. You can go ask him!"

"Tell me! Tell me! Does he know Him?" my son pleaded— and *not* in his indoor voice.

I sort of chuckled a little and said, "I don't know that man, and I don't know if he knows Jesus." I'll admit that I was nervous, and I wasn't sure why.

I gathered my stuff, keeping my daughter from dropping the Rice Krispies Mason jar on her head, picked up my food, found my keys, and said, "Okay, let's take our food to our house!" Meanwhile, my son was still shouting, "Does he know Him? Does he know Him? Tell me!" as we left. *Nothing to see here, folks!* I thought, darting my eyes and flashing a smile around the crowded room.

I buckled the kids into their car seats, put my food in the car, drove us home, unloaded everything, and got the food on the table. But as soon as I started eating my lunch, I got "that feeling." Truthfully, that feeling started the second my son asked the awkward question in the café, but it had intensified until I just couldn't stand it any longer. If you know Jesus, then you might remember this feeling from when you decided to give your heart to Him. It is that overwhelming sensation that will not quit until . . . you . . . ACT. I know this feeling as the nudging of the Holy Spirit—and He doesn't give up too easily. I mean if death couldn't stop Him, then I have a feeling that my lunch plans weren't going to either. You know what I mean?

So we were sitting there at my kitchen table when my son brought up the topic one last time: "Momma. We don't know if that man knows Jesus. We don't know if he is going to be in heaven with us."

And that was all it took. I picked up my keys and declared that we were going back to the café to see if that man was still there, and if he was, we would ask him if he knew Jesus. Friend, I love Jesus. I know lots about Him. I have encountered His love. I have seen His power. I have witnessed His work, but I have a confession. Even with all this love of God living inside of me and my intense desire to share the love of God with the world, I was *terrified when presented with my first real opportunity.*

I decided it would be a good idea to prepare my son for the encounter.

"Kolton, after we ask the man if he knows Jesus, the man might say, 'Yes! I know Jesus.' And we will say 'Jesus is my friend too!' And give him a high-five." I went on to say, "But he might say, 'No. I don't know Jesus.' What are we going to say to him then?"

Kolton thought for a minute, then answered matter-of-factly, "Well, Jesus knows him! He knows everybody! And He loves him very much!" My heart jumped a little. *Good answer,* I thought, but I prepped my son again. "So, if the man says, 'No. I don't know Jesus.' We are going to say . . . ?"

"He loves you very much."

"Okay, and if he says he *does* know Jesus?"

"We will give him a high-five!"

That was it. We were as ready as we could be. I loaded the kids into the car and started the three-minute drive back to the café. That feeling still wouldn't go away. It overwhelmed me. I really had no choice but to drive back. It sounds easy and simple—but it was a truly awesome feeling. And we are talking awesome as in . . . BIG. HUGE. SCARY.

Have you ever been asked by the Holy Spirit to step outside your comfort zone? Have you found yourself walking over to a stranger to offer help or saying a few kind words to your waitress because you felt led to do so? Did you feel nervous? I sure was, but surprisingly my son was not. Oh, to be like my little boy!

I glanced up to look at him in the rearview mirror. He was playing in the backseat with a dinosaur toy, and his biggest concern was whether he would get to bring it into the café with him once we arrived. But all I could think was, *Doesn't he know that we are about to approach a* stranger *and talk to him about* Jesus*?!*

I pulled up and parked directly in front of the door. I hopped out, knowing that I would be able to see from the front of my car if the man was still sitting there. Maybe he had gone home, and my faithfulness to drive back would show Jesus and my kids that I wanted to do what was right. Maybe I wouldn't have to actually speak to the man. But as I peered into the café window from the sunny sidewalk, I saw that he was still there . . . sitting at the same table . . . waiting for us.

I unloaded my kids from the car, then walked into the café. The man seemed a little unsure of why I was approaching him, and even though I knew that God had led me to talk to this man, I was still shaking as I started to speak. What I said next came out in about two seconds (evidence of my nerves): "Hi. My son was waving at you earlier. He came over to me and asked if you knew Jesus. He was really concerned that you might not. We couldn't finish our lunch at home until we came back up here so that we could ask you . . . So, do you?"

The man looked at me, a bit confused. Then he looked at my son and his yellow dinosaur toy, and he smiled. I don't know if he had tears in his eyes or if I was just looking through the ones in my own, but I will never forget what happened after that. This man swung his chair toward my son, leaned way down to look Kolton in the eye, and held out his hand.

"Buddy, come here. Give me a high-five . . . Jesus is my friend."

I wanted to cry. I wanted to bawl right there in the middle of that café. He had used the exact words that I had used to prepare my son. "Jesus is my friend. High-five." We couldn't have rehearsed it any better.

It was a moment that forever changed me, and it was the first time that I had shared the love of Jesus with the "world," and I got to do it as a mom! I wanted to tell everyone. I wanted to tell as many people as I could that sometimes simple acts of obedience produce the greatest faith. I wanted to tell them how God promises to meet us when we bravely do what He asks of us. I wanted to tell them that it's never too late to go back for the ones that God has placed in our path. And I wanted them to see that ordinary moments are always more when we act with God.

So I used the platform that I had available and posted that story to my fashion blog. And that is when everything changed.

As those who read my story online began to share it with their friends, I suddenly realized that maybe this is what God meant when He said that He was giving me an audience and I would be responsible for them. Maybe He had things that He wanted me to say—words that He was going to trust me to deliver safely. And suddenly my small world in the middle of nowhere Oklahoma got a little bit bigger.

That wasn't the last time that God asked me to approach a stranger, and it certainly wasn't the most challenging either. Over the course of the next six months, the Lord taught me what it meant to stop in the middle of my day and listen for how He might be leading me. This tuned my ears to hear His voice more clearly. And as I did what He asked, I learned about His faithfulness to meet us in our obedience. This became the message that I wanted to share with others. This became the truth that I had to say. I didn't want to use my blog to tell women, "Put on this shirt. It will make you feel good about yourself," but instead, "Put on this confidence of the power of a living God inside you, because He wants to use you to reach a hurting world." And through all of this, I realized that maybe I hadn't missed God or His plan for my life after all.

In that first year, my website was visited over ten million times and read in nearly every country across the globe. To me, this was the evidence of the faithfulness of God fulfilling what He had told me in the beginning, *"I'm going to give you an audience, and you will be responsible for them."* And so I did my very best to keep my end of that promise. I did my very best to be responsible for what God had placed on my heart to share.

And each time I wrote, it felt as if the same Holy Spirit who didn't give up until I went back to the café prompted me to keep reaching out to one mom, one wife, one woman who needed to be reminded that God loves her very much. And through all of it, I simply did what was asked of me, and God did the heart work and received all the glory.

And suddenly, I saw it. I saw what God had done.

All of the moments that didn't make sense before, all of the times that I was just sure that I had missed it following the wrong path, weren't mistakes or missteps. It became clear to me that everything I had believed was leading me away from God's plan was actually preparing me for it. Marrying Jared, moving to this small town, becoming a mother, and doing my best to follow the Lord's leading were all important pieces of the story that He was asking me to tell. I just hadn't seen the significance of those steps at the time. Jared didn't have to be a pastor. Our life together wasn't some plan B. There wasn't this track of God's perfect plan that ran parallel to my life that I would never be able to reach. I was right where the Lord had wanted me to be. He had known what He was doing all along, and He had gotten me to where He needed me. I just had to keep walking in faith.

GOD NEEDS YOU TOO

No matter how overlooked or forgotten you believe you are, what you are doing in this season of your life has significance. Whether you are home with little ones, working a job or three jobs, whether you are on your way somewhere or coming from somewhere . . . this time is not simply a waiting period until you get to whatever comes next. The place where you find yourself in this season is a significant part of your story.

So, friend, will you please do something for me? Will you stop reading these words and look around the room? Take it all in. The lighting. The sounds. How your heart feels at this exact moment. Now, listen to me. God wants you to know that He has you in the palm of His hand. You are not forgotten. You haven't missed God's plan for your life. And He cares about the desires of your heart. I don't care who has told you that your dream won't ever work out, that it is foolish or impossible, or that you are too young or too old. Scripture says in the psalms that we should delight ourselves in the Lord and He will give us the desires of our hearts.[2] I don't think it is saying that delighting in the Lord is our ticket to getting whatever we want. Rather, when we find delight in the Lord, He gives us the right desires. He places incredible dreams within us, and He is more than able to bring them to pass. We just have to be willing to trust His heart even when we don't understand this part of His plan. And sometimes it takes seven years and two entire chapters to see how it all unfolds.

Let's Talk

There is this scene in one of my favorite movies where the main character must step out in faith to save his dying father. Following the instructions in his father's notebook to find the medicine that will save his father's life, the main character is led to a large chasm. The hero knows that there is no way around it, and while he can't see anything in front of him, he knows that his father has guided him to this place—that there must be a way across the divide. He takes a deep breath, steps out in faith . . . and he doesn't fall. Instead, he finds himself standing on a narrow bridge connecting the two sides of the valley. It had been there all along, perfectly camouflaged to match the canyon wall. He just hadn't been able to see it before.

Friend, there are steps directly in front of you that will take you to where God is gently calling your heart. You might not be able to see it from where you are standing now, but there is a path that will take you to your purpose. And the moment that you step out, you will find yourself standing securely on God's Word.

What are some of the things that He is still calling your heart to do? Write them out here.

———————————————————————————————

———————————————————————————————

———————————————————————————————

When I was little, my elementary school was across the street from my house. One evening, my dad agreed to take me to the school's playground after work. I remember holding his hand before we crossed the busy road. After a few minutes, with cars coming and going from both directions, I wondered if there would ever be a break in the traffic.

I kept looking at the cars, then back at my dad. "Can we go now, Daddy?" But my dad just kept his eyes on the road, and his hand in mine. "Not yet, sweetheart. Not yet."

There are moments just like that in all of our lives. We can see where we want to be, but for some reason, we just can't get there yet. You know, it would be easy to question the Lord in those moments. It would be easy to want to rush Him. But just like my dad on that evening all those years ago, God also knows that timing is everything—and that eventually, you will get across the street safely.

So let Him worry about the road, the cars, and how the two of you are going to get to the other side, while you focus on your Father's face. Focus on how safe your hand feels tucked in

His. When you finally get to the other side, and you are free to run, you might just find yourself missing the time with your Daddy on the sidewalk.

What are some of the ways that you can focus on the Father as He prepares your path? Maybe you could spend time in the Word. As we listen to what the Father has already said to us, it helps us hear Him more clearly as He continues to speak. Another way to focus on the Father is to praise Him for what He has already done in your life. Reminding your heart of God's goodness stirs up faith as you believe Him to safely lead you into whatever else is to come—and to see purpose in where you are right now.

Can you think of a time when you felt you were on hold? Do you feel like that is where you are right now? If it was a previous time in your life, write out how the Lord moved you to the other side of the waiting. Or if that's where you feel you are right now, tell the Lord how you feel about this season, and then write out the things that you are still hoping for. He hears you, you know.

Let's Pray

Lord, we commit our lives and our plans to You. We trust that You aren't just good, but You are working things out for our good as well. Help us to follow You boldly. Help us to trust You completely. And help us to remember that You haven't forgotten about us. Above all, Lord, help us to remember that Your plans are always so much better than our own. Lord, I ask that You would reveal the areas in which we can begin to pursue the deeper desires of our hearts. Begin a conversation with us as we listen for where You are leading us next. In Jesus's name we pray, amen.

Let's Hope

God's timing is perfect. I will trust it, and I will trust Him because He is a faithful God!

3

A Fight for Joy

GOD IS GOOD EVEN WHEN LIFE ISN'T

Seven years ago, hope was fading and fear was taking over my newly pregnant heart. I had been in agony for almost a week. This was my first pregnancy, my first appointment with my OB-GYN was not scheduled for another month, and I couldn't get in to see anyone else. I had been calling relentlessly and had found no one to answer my questions: "Is this normal? Should this be happening?"

No one seemed to care that my baby might be dying.

I can well remember the day that I found out I was pregnant. I just had a feeling. We hadn't been trying . . . but we knew it was possible. I was at work, but I just couldn't wait until I got home to find out. So I asked a coworker if she happened to have a pregnancy test. Crazily enough, she had one with her. I mean, what are the odds? Being the wonderful friend that she is, and because we are girls and rarely do we go to the potty alone (even before we become mommas), she followed me into the bathroom.

"Well?" she asked anxiously from the other side of the stall.

As I flung open the door, I waved the stick and shouted, "Is that a second line? I think that's a second line!" I couldn't believe what the test seemed to be indicating, but the second and third tests I took later confirmed it. They were positive, and so was I.

I was pregnant.

I told my husband a few days later . . . on his birthday. Along with the usual birthday gifts, there was one special present—a bib that declared him "World's Greatest Dad." Oh, and I included the pregnancy test . . . because what guy doesn't want to hold something that you peed on? After the initial shock wore off, we laughed and cried, then I told him that I knew just how I wanted to tell our families. We would invite everyone for dinner to "celebrate his birthday," but we would give each of our parents a little present once they arrived. Continuing the trend, I bought four more little bibs—one for each of the world's greatest grandmas and the world's greatest granddads!

The day came, and we passed out the presents. I wish that we had taken pictures, because that moment of pure joy was one of a kind. It would be the last time that we would say, "We are pregnant," without the quiet little fear that whispers, *But what if it happens again?*

I was so proud as I called to schedule my first OB/GYN appointment. I was moving into the ranks of motherhood, a role I had dreamt of since childhood. The receptionist asked how far along I thought I might be. She told me that they didn't usually schedule the first appointment until around twelve weeks, so we set the appointment for early October. It was my first pregnancy, and so while I thought it was a very long wait, I didn't question their procedures. Back then I didn't realize that they waited to schedule the first appointment because the majority of miscarriages happen before twelve weeks.

Just a couple of weeks later, I woke up and instantly knew something was wrong—I was in pain. I remembered hearing that your body makes room for the baby and stretching can cause discomfort. But this was different. This was pain. Immediately, fear warned me what could happen next.

The phone rang five times before anyone answered. "Hello. This is Becky Thompson, and I am pregnant . . ." The person on the other end interrupted, asking for my date of birth.

"Yes, I know that my appointment isn't for another month, but—"

"No. I haven't been seen yet, but I am experiencing some discomfort, and there are some other indications that I might be losing the baby . . . I know that there are no available appointments. I was just wondering if this was an emergency or if I could speak with a nurse."

I left my name and number and prayed that someone at their office would return my call. I called my husband and my mom. None of us knew what to do next.

Three days went by with no response to my desperate messages and voicemails. No one seemed to care that I might be losing this baby. I felt helpless and unheard.

The bleeding had slowed, but it hadn't stopped. I was terrified, but I didn't have anyone else that I trusted to call. I guess I just thought that every doctor's office would act this way. I know better now.

I spent the next few days at home lying flat on the couch, as though I could stop what I feared the most. As I lay there, I prayed. I asked God to heal my body and protect my child. I told Him all about how I had made plans for this baby. I told Him that I had a girl's name picked out. She would be my sweet Kaylin Joy, and I desperately wanted to meet her.

When Hope Seems Lost

There is a story in the Bible that tells about King Nebuchadnezzar, who erected a large statue of himself and declared that all of the people must bow and worship it. Three men of God defied the king and were threatened with death. Their response? "If we are thrown into the blazing furnace, the God we serve is able to deliver us from it, and he will deliver us from Your Majesty's hand. But even if he does not, we want you to know, Your Majesty, that we will not serve your gods or worship the image of gold you have set up."[3]

But even if He does not . . .

I made the decision to live right there on those words. I parked my mind on the Truth that God would still be God even if He didn't answer me. I reminded myself that even if He did not save my baby, He was still able and good and worthy of my devotion. I resolved to focus on those words alone and not the words that fear whispered—the relentless *what-ifs*.

When the phone rang that Wednesday evening, a man's voice was on the other end. "Hello. I am returning a call for Becky Thompson. I am going to prescribe you some medicine for the pain and some medicine that you can take the next time you are pregnant to help you keep the baby."

In my hope, I refused to hear him.

"Thank you so much for calling me back! Do I need to come in?"

He continued, "No. It is likely that you are miscarrying. We will just be more proactive next time. In the meantime, I will get you started on some pain meds."

I cut him off. "Proactive? Next time? I have been lying flat on my back and calling for a week! You were supposed to call me back! I picked you to be my doctor. No, I have been nothing *but* proactive. I am not concerned with my next pregnancy. I am concerned with what needs to happen to keep *this* baby. Can you do anything to help me?"

I honestly do not remember what he told me, but at the end of the call, we had an appointment for an ultrasound the next morning.

That night, we prayed. We prayed harder than we have ever prayed. I laid my head against my husband's chest and cried out for God to save the life of my sweet baby. I pleaded for Him to intervene.

The pain the next morning was unbearable. My body trembled from it, and beyond the physical agony, my heart ached. Hope was fading, and the voice of fear seemed louder than ever. I looked out the window on the way to the hospital and thought back over the week. Maybe I could have done more. Maybe I could have called another doctor. Maybe this was somehow all my fault. I was exhausted and felt defeated . . . But I wasn't prepared for how I would feel once we arrived at the doctor's office.

My husband helped me through the door and guided me into a chair. As if the physical pain was not enough, the room was full of greatly pregnant women—women with hope in their eyes and joy in their hearts. I was a picture of hopelessness—fear was winning. *"You will never know that joy. It is over for you,"* it sneered.

They couldn't have called my name soon enough. I couldn't wait to get out of that room.

The nurses had no clue why I was there. Each one that entered congratulated me on my pregnancy. I told at least three different nurses that I thought I was losing the baby, that I had shown signs of it for a week, and that this appointment was to basically confirm my fears. None of them were prepared to counsel that. Who is?

The doctor came in, and I wanted to punch him. He was big and jolly and didn't seem to have any concern. I hadn't realized how angry I was with him. Why had he abandoned us? How could he have simply ignored our calls? Rationality played no part in this meeting or my feelings toward him. I needed someone to blame.

The screen came to life as the ultrasound began. "See that little sphere there? That is your baby." He continued, sounding a little surprised, "See that little flash? That is the baby's heartbeat."

Hope sprang to life inside of me!

"Your baby is still alive. I don't see why you shouldn't be able to take that medicine I prescribed and keep the child."

I cried and laughed, then I hugged and thanked him.

Suddenly my doctor was a saint. I walked out with my head raised and my heart focused on new life. I called all our friends and family. We had already told everyone about the pregnancy early, so now we shared our additional good news with our huge support team!

But as we left, something still didn't feel right. The pain had escalated and caused me to hold my breath and double over. (Three successful pregnancies later, I recognize it now as labor.) I told my husband that I would just keep making phone calls and stay in the car while he picked up our lunch.

We made one more stop, and the extreme tightening of my abdomen became intolerable. We rushed to get the pain medicine. I made the last "good news" call as my husband walked into the drug store to pick up my relief. And then . . . it happened.

Right there, in the parking lot of Walgreens, I felt the baby slip from my body.

When my husband returned to the car, he understood instantly what my lips couldn't say. I was frantic and just wanted to get to the hospital.

More phone calls. I dialed my mom and then Jared's. I sobbed hysterical words as I told them it was over. I have tried to remember what happened in those few minutes on the way to the hospital, but I was honestly in shock and remember very little of it.

I can tell you exactly what happened once we arrived at the hospital.

My husband helped me into the emergency room. I walked past the front desk and into a little bathroom. It was cold. I put the little egg-sized baby into a paper towel and carefully placed it in my purse. A wheelchair was waiting for me when I got out. I sat down and waited. My husband knelt beside me. My parents arrived. I sat longer. Apparently, almost an hour went by while I sat in a wheelchair with my baby in my purse. I began to feel lightheaded and numb. There was no privacy. But even privacy couldn't have provided what my heart needed. My baby was gone.

I was jolted back to reality by raised voices. My mom directed my husband to get the car and help me into it because we were done waiting. As we left, the hospital staff was well aware of how displeased we were.

We drove to another hospital near our home. I was immediately taken into an exam room, and the last words I heard my momma say as they wheeled me around the corner were, "Don't let them take the baby."

It was the first thing I told the nurse. "I want to keep the baby. You can't have it." I couldn't imagine my child being shipped off to some lab.

The nurse's soft words echoed in my heart, "Honey, what are you going to do with it?"

I couldn't answer her. I just sobbed. It wasn't just a mass of cells. It wasn't just tissue. It was my baby. It was hopes and dreams. It was a future and a life; it was my sweet Kaylin Joy.

And yet I knew the nurse was right. If they examined my baby, then maybe they would be able to tell me what had gone wrong. Maybe they could keep it from happening again. As I handed her my sweet little baby, suddenly a stillness came over me.

For the first time in over a week, it was quiet. There was no rushing. There was nothing left to fight for. I didn't have to convince someone I needed help. I didn't have to plead a case of desperation. Hope was gone. Fear was gone. My baby was gone. It was all over. My body that was designed to protect my child had betrayed it. I was cold. Numb. My baby had died.

When God made woman, He made her to bring forth new life. Yes, He made her to birth children, but He made her heart fertile as well. It is in the heart of a woman that dreams and visions are born. It is in a woman's heart that she makes plans for a future. I might dare say that the soft ground of a woman's heart is the most fertile thing about her.

At home, I slept for a long time. I was exhausted. The struggle had ended and left me shattered. It took a few days for my appetite and strength to return. But I was heartbroken. So I withdrew my hope and hid it away.

But what the Enemy intended for evil, the Lord has used

for good. As I withdrew hope, I pulled it back into the fertile ground of my heart. And there, without my knowing it, that hidden hope became a seed, and it began to grow again. That is the most powerful thing about hope, friend. Even if you only have a little, you have all that you need, because hope can't help but grow.

Have you ever been desperate to have a prayer answered? Have you ever brought your heart before the Lord and pleaded with Him to respond in a certain way, only for Him to seem silent? Those moments can shift our hearts away from believing the promise that we have a God who hears us and toward a panicked doubt that maybe God isn't as good as we thought. But the truth is, the sun can only stay hidden for so long before it begins to rise again, and hope can only stay buried for so long before it begins to bloom. But sometimes while we are waiting, the night can seem endless.

HOPE WILL RISE

When I was young, I suffered from night terrors. I would wake up in the middle of the night and find myself in a hazy place between sleep and consciousness, terrified of things that would never happen. I remember waking up one night in my momma's arms. I was crying hysterically, and she was singing softly to me. She brushed the hair off my face, saying, "Everything will be just fine, sweetheart. You will feel better in the morning. You will see that everything is right when the sun comes up." And she was correct. When the warm sun reached across the horizon, I always felt better. There is just something about being in light that makes everything a little more secure.

But there are some long nights, aren't there?

When we feel all alone—as if no one really understands what we are going through, when our relationship with our spouse seems uncertain, when the baby is sick and we don't know why, when the bills are piling up and we don't see how we will manage, when a beloved family member seems so helplessly broken—the night seems forever.

I have been in seasons of my life when it seems like the sun will never rise, when the darkness lingers, and when the warmth of the morning light seems unreachable. There have been seasons of my life when I believed the darkness and fear boasted of its success.

But those seasons do not last forever—no matter what the darkness whispers, no matter what our circumstances say. Even when fear promises that you will always feel this way—that you are never going to be truly happy again—the darkness cannot last forever because the sun always rises.

Always.

About a week after I lost the baby, I returned to my job at a

Christian university. Chapel service would be held that morning, and the faculty and staff were encouraged to attend. As the music began, I remembered my promise to myself and God. Even if He does not . . . He is still worthy; He is still good. And then a miracle happened. Hope began to unfold.

I told God exactly how I felt. I poured out my heart to Him. I told Him that I was heartbroken, but He already saw it. I told Him that I was discouraged, but He already knew it. I told Him that I still loved Him and that I knew He was still good, but I needed help to say it and He helped me to praise. He helped me hold up my arms and sing of His goodness and faithfulness. The words sprang up out of my heart, and I sang as though it was the only way I would keep breathing.

Praise became my weapon against grief.

I continued to praise because even though the baby had died, I couldn't lose my Jesus too. I couldn't believe that He had done this to me. I couldn't make Him the bad guy and blame Him, then run to find comfort and peace in Him. I needed Him more than ever, and when I called God good, I found peace. Because the truth is, He is good. Even when bad things happen, God is still good.

The goodness of God is unchanged by the brokenness of this world. He still loved me. He saw me in all of it, and He was right there with me. And He is with you too.

Joy Will Be Mine

The story about the three young men in the fiery furnace isn't just a narrative intended to highlight their devotion to God. It is proof of God's relentless dedication to us.

Because those three guys ended up in the flames. But when everyone looked inside, they didn't see ashes or smoke. Scripture says that when those on the outside looked into the flames, they saw a fourth man in the fire, and none of them were being burned. Friend, God doesn't promise that we won't walk through fire. But He absolutely promises that when we do, He will be with us.

I think that is my favorite part of that story in Scripture. While I am inspired by the fact that the men defied the king and declared their allegiance to God, and I am in awe of how they were not consumed by the fire, I am filled with so much hope because Jesus didn't leave them to face the flames alone.

I asked God to show me where He was when I felt as if I had been thrown into the flames, and He did.

He was right there with me as I discovered that I was pregnant. He shared in my joy. He was with me when the pain began, and He held me close. As frustrations led to desperation, He told me, *"I am here with you."* As fear whispered in the waiting room, *"You will never know that joy,"* He whispered,

"My daughter. That is a lie. Joy will be yours." He held me as that little life slipped into His arms. He wept with me at the brokenness of this world. He promised that the story wasn't finished and that one day I would meet my sweet baby in heaven.

And then, He gently put the broken pieces of my heart back together and filled it with a song as I remembered how to praise.

Friend, there is hope after miscarriage. There is hope after death. There is hope after devastation. There is hope when the prayer isn't answered. There is hope when the bills aren't paid and the baby is hungry. There is hope when your husband leaves and says he is done. There is hope during cancer. There is hope when the war is raging. Because there is hope in Christ alone, and He is with us through it all.

I don't know what you are going through right now. I don't know what you have just come out of, or what you are facing up ahead. But I know this, it is often easy to hear the voice of the Enemy when things go terribly wrong or when we experience deep hurts. Perhaps they are the same lies that the snake told Eve after her world fell apart and she had to leave the garden: "God doesn't love you. Look what He did to you. If He cared about you, you wouldn't have to go through this." But friend, when Jesus died, He made a way for us to be in a relationship with the Father again. He made a way for us to have His Holy

Spirit with us always, but we still live in a shattered world with the very real Enemy of our souls.

We must remember to tune our hearts to the voice of Truth inside of us that reminds us, *"I love you, my daughter. I weep at the brokenness of this world. I weep with you in your pain and suffering. But, dear one, I have made a way for you. I have made a way for you to overcome every trial and sorrow. I promise to never leave you. I promise that until the day I return, I will strengthen you. My heart is good, I am good, and My love for you is relentless."*

Visions from Heaven

At least once a year, I revisit this story of God's faithfulness during that season of my life. It is a time for me to praise Him again specifically for guiding me through such a painful time. I thank Him that I didn't lose my faith, but that through this, our relationship became deeper.

As I was praying one evening about five years after the miscarriage, I saw her. An image flashed before my eyes of a little brown-haired girl sitting backward in a chair pulled up to a big table. She looked a lot like my sweet Kadence, but she had a long, brown ponytail. She was about five years old, and my goodness, she was so beautiful.

Yes, the baby died well before we knew who she was, but I

believe with all of my heart that the Lord gave me a little glimpse into heaven. While there are times that my heart still aches to know my first child, there is no greater peace than the assurance that she is held safely in the arms of Jesus. The same arms that hold me today.

✎ Let's Talk

I push my kids on the swings in our backyard almost every evening—especially during the summer. Over the last few years, we have spent countless hours on those swings. I push, and they giggle and chat and kick their little feet, pretending to run through the air. I wouldn't trade the time that we have spent there for anything in the world. Those memories are priceless to me.

One day, I noticed that just behind their swings was a place on the ground where the grass had been worn thin. And I knew instantly, that's where Mommy was. You could clearly see the place where I had stood to push them on the swings.

And I know that this is a gift, because they won't always be able to see the places that I have been with them. But even though there might not always be physical evidence to show that I have been with them, with every moment, with every string of minutes-turned-memories, I am wearing a familiar place in their hearts. A place that they will be able to look back on and say, "That's where my Mommy was."

And the same is true for our heavenly Father. Yes, there are places in our lives where we can say, "See? This is where God showed up. This is where we sang and talked and laughed and where He pushed me a little higher." And we celebrate the assurance of His presence. But even in the places where He is not as visible, where we cannot see the evidence of His footprints in the grass as clearly, we can be confident that He has been with us all along. We can sense His familiar workings in our hearts and know that even in the unseen moments, our heavenly Father was there too.

So, friend, I know there are places in your heart and parts of your story that are hard to revisit. I know there are moments where you say He is good, but your heart wonders, *"But where were You?"* Before we go on, I'd like you to ask Him, *"Where were You, Lord, in that specific season? Where were You when I was lost or scared or lonely? Where were You when I was hurt and broken and desperate?"*

Where are some of the places that you have questioned the Lord's presence in your life? Did an event leave you questioning His goodness? Did pain or trauma convince your heart that He had abandoned you? It is a powerful thing to look back into those places and ask the Lord where He was when those events were happening.

Take some time and ask Him to show you exactly where

He was when you needed Him the most. And, friend, I want you to listen for His voice as He tells you exactly where He was. Because the truth is, He was with you through it all. And when we trust that He was with us through those times we doubted, we can be confident that He has been and will be with us through all that is to come. Write out what the Lord says or what He reveals to your heart.

_____

_____

_____

❦ Let's Pray

Lord, we trust You. It is our confession, God. Sometimes, our mouths have to say the words that our hearts aren't quite ready to believe. Because, Lord, it's hard to believe those words of faith sometimes—to say that we really trust You. Trust means that we are giving something of ourselves in exchange for what You have to offer. We give away our doubt. We give away our fear. We give away our insecurities. In exchange, Lord, we believe that You will come through for us. We believe that You have been with us through it all, and we believe that Your love is what has held us together in even our most uncertain times. Bring healing to the areas of our hearts where we feel wounded.

Bring confidence to our hearts as we trust in Your faithfulness. And help us believe what we so desperately want to remember: You are good. In Jesus's name we pray, amen.

Let's Hope

God did not abandon me in my pain. He was with me, even when I was unsure of His presence. Because His goodness is eternal, I will choose to praise Him!

4

Is It Just Me?

YOU'RE NOT ALONE

If the city was so great, then why don't you just go back there?"

Her words hung in the air over my thirteen-year-old head. *If only I could,* I thought. *I would move home in a heartbeat.*

I was in the seventh grade, and it was my first year of school in Paoli, Oklahoma—population 705. That's 705 people—just in case you were wondering. Not the number of stop signs or convenience stores. That number represents the entire population of the town. (I fully expected them to change the sign after we arrived, and I was disappointed when they didn't.) We moved to town after my dad was appointed to be the new pastor for the Methodist church. It was our first adventure: we were leaving Oklahoma City to minister in a small town. I remember being excited when my parents told me that we were leaving everything that we had ever known. Yes, I realize how strange that might seem, but I remember clapping and cheering because it was something different. For a girl who had grown up at the same school with the same friends and the same church in the same city for her entire life, moving didn't sound scary. I looked at the change as a brand-new adventure. And I had always wanted to go on an adventure.

The first time I saw Paoli was the day that the moving truck followed our car to our new house. I remember pulling into town for the first time and immediately feeling *much less excited*. As a matter of fact, I wondered just what we had gotten ourselves into. There are small towns like the one that I live in today, and there are small towns like that tiny town. There was one gas station. There was one high school building and a few stop signs. There were a few churches and a few houses, and that was it. To top it off, the small parsonage where we lived sat on the church property, and Momma always joked that she could take a shower and wave at the people in worship at the same time. We laugh about it now, but like everything else in town, there wasn't much privacy either.

But being the eternal optimist that I am, even back then I was determined to make the best of the whole thing. Starting a new school in a new place was like being given a blank slate. I could be anyone I wanted to be, and I had five weeks to decide. No one at this school knew me as Becky, the ten-year-old girl who still brought her American Girl doll with matching outfit to school (true story). They would only know what I wanted them to know. I could be any version of myself that I wanted: edgy or bubbly or sporty or anything in between. (Actually, let's be honest: sporty was never going to happen. I am the least coordinated person that I know—I run like Woody from *Toy Story*.) So, after much deliberation, I decided that I would just play it cool. I would just blend in. I would be laid-back, fun-to-be-around, super-chill Becky . . . who would obviously leave her doll at home.

When the first day of school came, I was more like nervous, anxious, let-me-go-home (like-all-the-way-back-home-to-Oklahoma-City) Becky.

I was also terrible about blending in. I don't know why, exactly. It could have been the hundred glittery butterfly clips that I wore in my hair (some were motion clips that bounced when I walked) or my recent, parentally approved, glitter eye shadow. But let's just say, people noticed me.

It turned out that even though I had spent most of the summer alone, everyone knew who I was once I got to school. They were curious about the new girl, and so they asked questions. I have to be honest, I felt a little important. (Okay, I was basically a celebrity—by Paoli standards.) I enjoyed telling them about myself and talking about how different life was in the city. It made me feel interesting—like I was someone worth getting to know, who had stories to tell that were worth hearing.

Until that one afternoon just after lunch . . .

A bunch of people were sitting around waiting for the next period to begin. I was finally starting to feel less like an outsider and more like one of the group. I was finally starting to think that maybe this whole new town/new friends thing wasn't going to be so intimidating after all. I remember feeling brave as I jumped into the middle of the conversation. To be honest, I'm not sure what I said exactly, but I know it started with, "Well, in the city . . ." And that's when one of my new friends had heard enough. She didn't want to listen to one more story about where I had come from or what I had done. And while I can't remember her name or what she looked like, I can remember her words: *"If the city was so great, then why don't you just go back there?"*

And all at once, I felt so very, very alone.

All I had were my stories. I was made up of all of the moments leading up to that one. If they didn't want to hear about who I was before, then what could I even talk about? What would I have to share? And the things that really mattered to me, and the things that made me . . . well, me . . . Well, it felt like no one wanted to hear about them either. That afternoon, surrounded by dozens of people, I realized that true loneliness doesn't only come from being by yourself. There is another type of loneliness that comes from not being known. A loneliness that takes place when others see you, but they don't see *you.*

And that was a feeling that I thought I wouldn't ever have to experience again.

Until I became a momma.

Nobody Said It Would Feel Like This

I went into labor with my oldest child, Kolton, six years ago in the aftermath of an Oklahoma snowstorm. These storms don't happen often, but when they do, they're memorable. It was Christmas Eve, and the major interstate highways were shut down, people were stranded alongside roadways, thousands were without power and heat, and this soon-to-be momma was having contractions and pacing her living room.

I kept telling my husband, "You're going to have to dig us out, you know. You're going to have to go out in this blizzard and make sure that we can get out of the driveway if we need to go tonight, because I am *NOT* prepared to have this baby at home." There are brave, beautiful, amazing women out there who choose to have their babies at home. There are women who dedicate their lives to helping other women make this a safe reality. But a home birth was not a part of my birth plan. As a matter of fact, as my due date got closer, my birth plan had two important parts:

1. Make it to the hospital.
2. Have baby.

You can see why the three feet of snow that we woke up to as I had steady contractions at nearly thirty-seven weeks of pregnancy was cause for concern. This amount of snow might not be notable for some parts of this country. But for us? Well, let's just say I'll never forget my sweet husband with his little shovel, hour after hour, making sure that we had an evacuation route down the driveway and into the street if we needed it. We hadn't quite determined how we were going to make it out of the neighborhood, but somehow we did.

That snow was still on the ground when we brought Kolton home from the hospital just a few days later. As a matter of fact, it wasn't until all of the visitors went home and my husband went back to work that I remember the ice finally beginning to thaw. I remember sitting in the nursery one afternoon rocking Kolton and listening to the whispered drips of melting ice outside the window, hoping that the sun would do the same for me. I hoped that it would melt away the mountain of fears that consumed my heart.

Later that night, after Jared came home from work, my parents came over to hold the baby. We all sat around staring at our tiny, sleepy gift and taking in the wonder of new life, when all of a sudden I just couldn't contain my fear anymore. Jared was talking about some television show, and I cut him off and blurted out, "Being a mommy is so lonely!"

My sweet husband just looked at me. He didn't know what

to say. Well, no one really knew what to say. My own momma tried. "Honey, it is perfectly normal to feel overwhelmed."

But the irony of that moment isn't lost on me. I was surrounded by the people who love me the most, who just wanted to help in any way that they could, and I was announcing that I felt all alone.

I had made a powerful admission. It is a truth that I think many of us experience but few of us ever give voice to. I had been a momma for just a few days, and I had already discovered this reality: motherhood is lonely.

Do you ever feel lonely? Maybe you are a single mom, and you play the role of both parents. You work all day, parent all evening, and worry 24/7 that somehow you're not going to be enough. Or maybe your husband is often away—maybe he works away from home, or is deployed in the armed forces, or just seems as if he isn't as emotionally invested as you want/need him to be. You feel the weight of the family on your shoulders, and you desperately wish you had a partner whom you could count on to help carry the load. You feel like you're doing it all by yourself. You just wish for a free minute when you could stop being in charge. Or maybe you're surrounded by people all day, yet somehow it feels like no one really knows you or understands you. Friend, it's not just you.

Because even on the days when you feel as though you have done it all by yourself. Even on the hard days when you just want help and there is no one to ask. Even on the days when you just don't know how you're going to keep going, the Lord has been with you and will continue to be with you.

In the previous chapter, we talked about asking the Lord where He was during the significant moments in our lives, but there is something else we need to talk about. Yes, God is there in the major moments, but He doesn't just show up for special occasions. He's not the type of guy who says, "I can't make it, but take pictures for me and show me later." God is with us in the most ordinary parts of our day. That thread of His presence that ties all of our moments together weaves through each one, leaving none untouched by His grace.

Scripture reminds us that He is the beginning and the end.[4] And friend, I think He must also be everything in between.

That means this moment isn't new to Him. He has already walked through everything we will face and knows just where to tell us to place our feet. Scripture says that the steps of a righteous person are ordered of the Lord,[5] and I believe that this is not only because God walks them with us but because He has gone before and prepared the path so that we can walk it together safely.

And if all of that is true, then that mountain in front of you—whether it is weeks of sleepless nights, a job change or a move, or a troubled relationship; or whether it is a surgery, a deadline, or a secret fear—sweet friend, God's already been to the other side of it. Not only is He going to lead you safely through it all, He is also going to guide you, as the One already waiting for you on the other side.

WELL-PLACED HOPE

So if Jesus is always with us, where do we look for Him? Well, I suppose the simplest answer is "everywhere." And while it seems like a very general statement, when we really stop to consider it—when we stop to think that the Savior of the world wants us to encounter Him in the middle of our day, wherever we are—it can revolutionize our thinking and empower our hearts.

Because one encounter with Jesus will change our lives forever.

There is this woman described in Scripture as the Samaritan woman. She isn't named, but she is identified by her nationality. This actually tells us a lot about her. The Samaritans had once been Jews. They knew all about the coming Messiah. They knew the Jewish law. But they had intermarried with people of other faiths. They had brought new gods into their land, and as a result, they knew that they would be excluded when the Messiah came. They also knew where they stood in the eyes of the Jews.

One afternoon, this Samaritan woman went to draw water from the well, and when she arrived she found a Jewish man sitting on the wall of the well. She didn't think much of it and went about her business. Suddenly this man speaks to her:

"Will you give me a drink?". . . .

The Samaritan woman said to him, "You are a Jew and I am a Samaritan woman. How can you ask me for a drink?" (For Jews do not associate with Samaritans.)

Jesus answered her, "If you knew the gift of God and who it is that asks you for a drink, you would have asked him and he would have given you living water."[6]

Given her heritage, this Samaritan woman was not a stranger to Jewish teachings, which said that there would be a Messiah who would come and save His people. But she was not a Jew, and so salvation would not be coming for her. At least, that is what she thought until that afternoon when Jesus spoke to her.

Jesus talked to her about the things going on in her home. He spoke to her about some of the things that likely weighed the heaviest on her heart, and then all of a sudden, something inside of her clicked. She realized that He was not like every other Jewish man.

How did He know so much about her? How did this man know exactly what she needed to hear? And then she said to Jesus (almost like more of a question than a statement):

"I know that Messiah" (called Christ) "is coming. When he comes, he will explain everything to us."

Then Jesus declared, "I, the one speaking to you—I am he."[7]

I love what this Samaritan woman does in response. She doesn't say one more word to Jesus at this point. She doesn't waste any time at all. Scripture says, "Then, leaving her water jar, the woman went back to the town and said to the people, 'Come, see a man who told me everything I ever did. Could this be the Messiah?' They came out of the town and made their way toward him."[8]

Scripture goes on to tell us that her entire community came to know Jesus because of her encounter with Him that afternoon.

I love so much about this story, and there are so many beautiful truths we could spend time discussing. But my very favorite part of what took place that day has to do with timing. I have heard that most women didn't go to draw water in the afternoon—they usually went in the morning when it was cool. But for some reason, this woman went out in the middle of the day, when she expected no one else would be there, and that is exactly when Jesus met her.

I love to imagine Jesus's face as this woman approached Him. Because He's Jesus, and that means He not only saw her coming that afternoon but He also had seen that moment coming from the beginning of time. I believe that when the earth was still being formed, when the Lord was still sculpting the seas and oceans and mountains in His hands, He already saw His encounter with the Samaritan woman. He already knew the outcome, and as she walked up to Him in the middle of her ordinary day, I'd like to think that He smiled, thinking, *I've been waiting for you!* He must have been filled with joy, knowing that she was about to discover the only One who could satisfy her heart and give her true hope.

He was just sitting on the wall of the well, waiting for her . . . at the exact place she would be . . . at the exact time she would be there . . . just to have an encounter with her.

And, friend, He does the same for you. He sees you coming. He knows everything about you, and He loves you just the same. Sometimes, the busyness of our day keeps us from looking for Him, but He is waiting for you, friend. He positions Himself in your life so you can meet Him face to face just when you need Him the most. And when you encounter Jesus, your heart will learn the gentleness of His voice, and it will be impossible to miss His presence again.

Listen to the Father speak hope to your heart. Listen to Him remind you that He will not leave you nor forsake you. He will not abandon you. Just as you show your little ones the way, He guides your hands and your heart, teaching you, His child. When you thought that you were all alone, He was with you. When you were convinced that He was far off, He held you tightly. Whatever is up ahead, you can face it together. Whatever is just over that horizon, He's got you covered. Because in Him there is love, peace, joy, health, wholeness, protection—and everything else that you might need. And He is with you always. Because Jesus doesn't just love the little children. He loves their mommas too.

❧ Let's Talk

It happened less than a year ago. Still trying to find my footing as a mom of three, I was just having one of those days where everything seemed impossible. Ever had a day like that? Nothing seems to go right, and there doesn't seem to be anyone to listen to everything that feels wrong? I called my husband at work, but he was up against a deadline and couldn't talk. I tried my best friend, but she wasn't answering—neither was my mom. I sat down on the floor of the living room and cried. No one was hurt. Nothing was broken. I just felt overwhelmed, and not having anyone to talk to about it somehow seemed to magnify my feelings.

It was then that my sweet five-year-old boy came over and sat down next to me and said, "I love you, Momma. Let's pray."

My goodness! That kid is something else. And he whispered a few simple words, "Jesus, help Momma. Amen." And I have never been more sure of the presence of the Lord than when my son invited Him to come close in that moment.

No matter the state of your circumstances, it is easy to feel as if no one else understands, friend. It is easy to feel all alone. But we know the truth that the Lord is always with us. In the previous chapter we discussed the moments where God felt far away. Have you ever experienced a time when you were certain that God was with you? When?

_____

_____

_____

❧ Let's Pray

Lord, we are some tired mommas! We work and we love, and we do it all to the best of our abilities, but some days, we feel overwhelmed by all of it. We feel like we are alone in the trenches. So, Lord, will You just come right now? Will You surround me and my new friend here with Your love? Will You make this a moment that we can point to with certainty and say that You were with us? Heavenly Father, we love You. We love Your Son, and we love Your Holy Spirit. Fill our hearts with hope as You remind us that You will never leave us. In Jesus's name we pray, amen.

❧ Let's Hope

I am not unseen. I am not forgotten. And I am *never* alone because God is always with me.

5

You Can't Do It All

LET GOD BE YOUR STRENGTH

When I was in high school, I had this odd summer job. Most teens work at the pool or the mall or a coffee shop. I did not. My summer job takes us back to the early 1900s and the first days of Oklahoma statehood. That sounds like every sixteen-year-old's dream. Right?

My mom worked as the director of a museum in downtown Oklahoma City, and she hired me to help with the summer tourist traffic. Now I say "museum" and "traffic," but what I want you to imagine are acres and acres of land nestled in the middle of a downtown Oklahoma City neighborhood where an historic Victorian house, a farm house and barns, and a one-room schoolhouse, all authentic to the early 1900s, had been moved onto the property and restored so that visitors could walk through and experience life as it was one hundred years ago.

During the school year, children from the local elementary schools would come and spend the day in the one-room schoolhouse and work in the garden. But during the summer, when schools stopped visiting, the museum had a steady trickle of daytime visitors who happened to find their way to the property from a tourist map.

My job was to take care of these tourists—all five of them. Okay, there were more than five, but the museum was tucked behind the state capitol, and at that time, very few people actually knew that it existed. Which meant there weren't too many people required to run the place.

It was a simple job, and most days I worked alone. When visitors arrived, I would leave the office and greet them at the welcome center/gift shop. I would hand them a map of the property and tell them that tours of the main house were offered on the hour, and their tour guide would meet them on the front porch. (I always thought this was sort of funny because it wasn't like we were waiting for other tourists to show up, and most of the time each family got their own tour.)

After the tourists left the gift shop, I would follow them out, lock the door, and then go to the back of the main house and get dressed into my costume for the tour. Yes. Costume. Over my work uniform of a polo shirt and shorts, I would pull on this long, pioneer-days dress with lots of layers and frills and lace. (I did mention this was in the middle of an Oklahoman summer right? It was hot. And by hot, I mean the surface of the sun would have seemed like a cool retreat.) Most of the time, I kept wearing my tennis shoes under that giant dress, and my hair was always in this messy, sweaty pony tail.

I would imagine the conversations that I would have with my friends upon returning to school at the end of summer break. "What did you do while school was out? Oh? You hung out by the pool and spent your free time at the mall? That's cool. What did I do? Basically the same thing." In my head I would add, *If by the pool you mean the pooling sweat in my Skechers under my prairie dress. Sweet Jesus in heaven, may they never learn the full truth.*

Anyway, no matter how long the people had been patiently waiting on the front porch of the house for their tour to begin, at the start of each hour, I would open the door and greet them. And all summer long, every time I opened that door, they were always surprised I was the one giving the tour.

I had that tour script memorized. I could give a good tour in thirty to forty-five minutes. When it was over, I would go into the back room, take off my dress, head out the back door, and try to beat the tourists to the barn where I would grab two ears of dried corn and then give demonstrations of antique corn grinders or washboards. And before they left? I was the one at the gift shop waiting for them. No matter where those visitors went, I was there waiting for them when they arrived, and it was my job to act like it was the first time that I had seen them all day.

"Well, hello, folks! So good to have you here today! Come on in, it's just about time for our tour to begin." "Oh, hey guys! I am just about to show how early settlers cleaned out the barn. Would you like to take this rake and give it a try?" And I know that they were thinking, *Wait. Wasn't she just . . . ? How'd she even get here so fast?*

But honestly, as a mom, I totally feel the same way. I feel like I have a job that requires me to be everything to everyone. From the moment I hear the alarm go off (aka baby crying), I know that I'm needed and that life won't pause for a moment until they all go to bed. (And even then, I'm still not off duty.)

You need breakfast? I will be your chef! *Clean clothes?* Fortunately, our launderer is on duty today. *The baby is bored?* Let's find you something to do, baby. *You need a doctor?* I'll get us an appointment! *You need someone to take care of your well-being, fun, education, amusement, social and emotional and spiritual adjustments to life?* I've got it all covered.

And while I'm at it, I will go ahead and balance marriage, friendships, caring for myself, and keeping up with our house, my job, and all of my other responsibilities. Also, I will do it all with excellence. I will do it all with the confidence that I'm not going to let anyone down. Except . . . *not really.* Except, *not at all.*

Because most days, I feel like my attention and heart are so spread thin that no one gets the best of me. It seems as if no one gets the love they deserve. And if I'm being completely honest, it is my marriage that I worry about the most.

BEFORE I WAS MOMMY, I WAS HIS

When we found out that we were pregnant with Kolton, my husband and I became one of those "new parent" couples. We researched together, shopped together, and made every choice related to the arrival of our new baby together. I'm talking right down to the discussion of which wipes would represent the Thompson household. (We went with Pampers if you were wondering.) If there was an *Amazing Race*–like show that somehow incorporated preparing for a new baby, we would have been all over that. We were a team.

To greater prepare ourselves for our baby boy's arrival, we even took one of those courses for new parents offered by the hospital.

The class and the instructor couldn't have met our expectations more perfectly. The sweet gal who led the class was spritely, informative, and gave entirely too-detailed descriptions of her own deliveries. After learning everything from diaper changes to natural labor techniques, our eight-week course ended with a certificate and a hospital tour of labor and delivery. We were prepared to become parents. We had the paper with our names written in Sharpie to prove it.

But what wasn't covered in that course, what would have been infinitely more valuable than any information we received in those few weeks, was the offering of a few simple words. If only our instructor had sat us down and said, "Ladies, before you were Mommy, you were his. Men, before you were Daddy, you were hers. Remember this. Hold on to this. Keep these words precious to you."

I wouldn't have understood her. I might not have even understood her a few months later. But four years down the road, I would replay those words over and over in my heart, and I would know exactly what she had meant.

So if I could teach that class, if I could go back and instruct the bright-faced, greatly pregnant women and their overly eager husbands, I would say this:

Ladies, there will come a day when your husband walks in the door and you do not turn around. You will be preoccupied with filling up sippy cups and wiping booties. You will shout over the running bath water, "Hey! Glad you're home." But it won't mean what it used to mean. It won't be full of eager anticipation to spend time together. It will be full of expectation that he will aid in meeting the demands of the family. "Glad you're home" will more properly translate as "Thank God for two extra hands to help me" and "Praise the Lord I might get five minutes alone now."

Ladies, there will come a day when you spend every last ounce of yourselves on your children. The demands of life and the babies will come before everything else. What little of yourself you have left at the end of the day will be used to crawl into bed before someone wakes up . . . and needs you again. The thought of doing anything else after the children are asleep will sound impossible, and your handsome husband's happy smile had better mean he is willing to get up with the baby and nothing more.

The husband that once completed your heart will be just one more person who needs you. The charming things that you fell for will go unnoticed. The daily grind will become expected.

Men, there will come a time when that beautiful bride sitting next to you hasn't showered in days. She will be at her wit's end, wearing other people's food and poop on her clothing. She will need to hear that she is beautiful, but she won't listen to you. She will need to know that she is still lovable, but she won't want you near her. When you arrive home after meeting the demands of work, you will be expected to meet the demands of your family. Your wife will hear none of your exhaustion, and you will see none of hers.

Men, you will call home to ask a quick question and anticipate a two-minute conversation. Half of it will be spent listening to your wife talk to your kids. As a matter of fact, you will make it no more than a few sentences into any conversation ever before your wife blurts out directions to your children: "Don't climb that!" or "Don't sit on your sister!" You will become accustomed to these outbursts, and you will forget that there was ever a time when you had her full attention.

But, ladies, when Mommy becomes your name, remember this man. Remember that you are his wife. Remember how much you love and appreciate him in this moment. Remember his dedication to your family. Remember his love and devotion to you. And then, when the days are long and you need a break, fall into his arms.

Men, remember your bride. The care and love that she has given you will soon be poured into your children. Her love for you will not change. Give her the grace to be enough even when she doesn't feel like it. Remember when your days are long, hers are too. Remember her. Fall in love with her again.

Remember each other. Remember the two that

made the family. Let the Lord lead you both together. Because when the days are endless and the hours short, it will be only His love that keeps you together. It will only be His mercy that gently guides your hearts as one. Hold tightly to one another, and even more tightly to the Lord. There is no greater adventure for you to experience and no greater gift than to walk through parenthood with your best friend. You are a team. Every single day.

Nearly ten years of marriage and six years of motherhood later, I cannot tell you how much I wish that someone had prepared me with this advice. Because the reality of balancing life as both a mom and a wife is overwhelming most days.

And knowing what I know now, I still find myself wondering, *How do I show my husband that I still love him when there is nothing left of me to give at the end of the day? How do I keep pouring out when I don't have anything left? And is there a way for this to change?*

The truth is, there is a way to begin to operate out of an overflow instead of on fumes, because the Lord desires that we live feeling fulfilled and not low-fueled. We just need to condition ourselves to stop and fill up before we run out, and we need to admit that trying to make it on our own will only lead to burnout.

BEFORE THE LIGHT COMES ON

I put gasoline into my car because my car needs gasoline to run. Period. This is one of the few facts that I am sure of when it comes to my vehicle. I am not a mechanic. (I know, you're surprised, aren't you?) And I am not one of those amazing women who knows all about cars either. But I do know that if I want my car to continue to do what it was designed to do—drive me to Target . . . I mean transport us around town—then it requires gasoline to do so.

Unfortunately, I also know that if the low-fuel light comes on in my car, then I can drive at least twenty-five more miles before I run out completely. Am I proud that I know this? Not exactly. But I must confess that more than once I have shouted into the backseat, "Okay, kids! Let's pray and ask Jesus to help us make it back into town! We're out of gas!" I like to think that I'm being some crazy kind of brave when I do that. Some women jump out of airplanes, while others deep-sea dive. Me, I go twenty-five miles on Empty. Scandalous.

But when I do stop to fill up, I do not put apple juice, water, or an energy drink into my gas tank because that's not what my vehicle needs. It needs gas.

And just as my car needs gasoline, I need the Spirit of God at work in my life to function properly. Because when God made us, He made us to find our completion in Him. He created us to require—yes, *require*—a relationship with Him in order to operate correctly. He didn't design us so that we could live life fully without Him. Your heart is designed to require a continual fellowship with the Father so that He can be the source of your strength. And in the depths of a woman's heart, something about this truth resonates.

This is one of the lessons that we can learn from the conversation that our friend, the Samaritan woman, had with Jesus. Remember? Jesus met her at the well, then spoke Truth into her heart: "Everyone who drinks this water will be thirsty again, but whoever drinks the water I give them will never thirst. Indeed, the water I give them will become in them a spring of water welling up to eternal life."[9]

He knew that she wasn't just in need of water to drink. She was in need of fuel for her soul. She needed the strength to face each day with the hope of Christ inside of her. She not only needed to be near Him, but she also needed Him to work through her. She needed His love to fill up her tank.

Free Fruit

Scripture describes what happens when God operates through us as the fruit of the Spirit. Just like the fruit a tree produces tells us what type of tree it is, we can tell when we are cultivating a relationship with Jesus by the fruit that our lives produce.

Scripture describes these fruits as love, joy, peace, patience, kindness, goodness, faithfulness, gentleness, and self-control.[10] When we see these attributes present in our lives, we can be confident that God is at work within us and through us.

But I want you to think about yesterday. Maybe the baby woke up early, and you didn't get the well-rested start you wanted. Or maybe the kids weren't in the best mood as they left for school. Maybe beginning the day a step behind has made you feel as if you're trying to catch up—running toward a goal that seems to always be sliding just a little bit farther away. The end of the day finally arrived, and you fell into bed—but there wasn't anything left. You had run out. You didn't have the time or the energy to give yourself or your spouse any attention. There just wasn't any love or any energy or any grace left in your tank.

Friend, if we are going to be continually pouring out the contents of our hearts as we care for those around us, then we must stay rooted in the Source of the fruit of the Spirit. Not the fruit of Becky or the fruit of your hard work.

You know, I have read many articles that say if you want to have a better relationship with your spouse, you need to do x, y, and z. If you want to have more patience with your kids, you need to do x, y, and z. And if you want more peace in your home, then you need to do x, y, and z. And many of those ideas just might work. They might produce temporary joy, temporary love, and temporary peace. But they will run out. Love and patience and peace that we try to manufacture with our own hands will always run out because these things aren't coming from the overflow of our hearts.

We are just like the woman at the well who went every day carrying a heavy jar back and forth just to get to the next day. No matter how much she carried away from the well, when it ran out, it was gone. She got what she needed and left. But Scripture says that when she realized that Jesus was the Christ, the Savior of the world, she left her jar and went back to the city from which she came. She told everyone she knew.

She had arrived at the well *carrying* the jar to fill up with temporary resources, but she left *as* the vessel that spilled out the Truth of Jesus, the Messiah, on everyone she encountered. What a beautiful picture of our own lives!

We are just going about our business, trying to be everything to everyone, trying to make it on our own, when Jesus shows up and reminds us that He is our source. He is our strength. He is the life and the love that we pour out on those around us. He is the peace that fills our homes. He is the joy that unites our families. He is the love that binds us together. And when we allow Him to be this source, we never run out.

So what does that look like exactly? What does it look like to stay filled up so that we love out of an overflow?

Well, sometimes, it looks like remembering that you don't have to do it all alone.

✤ Let's Talk

My daughter Kadence has dozens of tiny plastic Disney princess dolls. Each of them comes with a couple of clip-on dresses. We started collecting them a few years ago, and somehow we ended up with . . . well . . . more than any child should ever have, to be honest. Basically, they are like the Hot Wheels cars of the girly world. We just keep buying them even though I know we have buckets full at home. It's ridiculous. Unless you are my daughter, and then it is awesome.

One night at bath time, she decided that she wanted to take a bath with all of them. So, as I ran the bath water, she ran to find her girls.

I heard her bare feet walking on the wood floor as she came down the hall. She would take a step, I would hear a small *clack!* and then she would take another step and repeat. All the way down the hall until she finally reached the bathroom.

I poked my head out the door and realized immediately what had been making all of the mystery sounds. My daughter had arms full of dozens of tiny plastic dolls precariously positioned all the way up to her neck. And as she walked, one at a time would fall. She would stop, bend down to pick it up, and just as she did, another would fall from the top of the pile.

"Um. A little help here?" she said.

And after I took a quick picture on my phone (Just kidding. What parent would leave their kid struggling to take a picture first? *Points to self*), I tried to take her dolls from her.

"Let me help you, sweet girl!"

But a funny thing happened. She let me pick up the dolls that fell, but she wouldn't let me carry all of them for her. With arms still full, she waddled all the way to the bathtub and dropped them in, proud that she had only needed a little bit of help.

I wonder if we don't do the same thing. Rather than stay close to Jesus and let Him carry it all for us, we often just give Him some of it. "Here, Jesus. You can hold the things that I can't, but I can clearly manage the rest of this on my own." When really, we should just give Him everything.

Friend, He doesn't want you to become exhausted. He doesn't want you to feel overwhelmed. But sometimes, that means giving Him control of every area of your life. If Jesus were to speak to your heart right now, if He were to bend down, look you in the eyes, and say, "Let Me carry it all. Let Me help you," what do you think would be the hardest thing to put into

His hands? Why do you think it would be hard to give this over to Him? On the other hand, what one area given over to the Lord would provide the most relief?

_____

_____

_____

🌿 Let's Pray

Now, Lord, we know that You only speak kindly to us. We thank You that Your words are sweet and that Your love is abundant. Lord, the Samaritan woman taught us that when we are filled with Your love, all we want to do is give it away. She taught us this when she went to the well carrying the jar to be filled with water, and after encountering You, she left her jar and went back as the vessel of living water to be poured out on everyone she knew. Lord, help us to be more like her. Help us to remember that the more time we spend speaking with You in our hearts, the more of You will come overflowing from us into the lives of others. Lord, help us change our thinking. Help us remember that we were designed to be carriers of Your love and ambassadors of Your grace. Help us to cling tightly to You as we peel away the belief that there is any kind of glory in doing it all on our own. And finally, help us to see that when we admit our dependence upon You, You are glorified as the One who is able above all to help us. It's in Jesus's name that we pray these things, amen.

❧ Let's Hope

God is my Source. God is my Strength. I will not forget that I can do all things through Him alone.

6

Real Life Looks Lived In

YOU ARE NOT YOUR MESS

So, here's the thing. I'm sure there are things that you might expect to read in a book. There are certain stories that would seem as though they are appropriate to share in order to make a certain point, or convey a certain message. But I need to be real for just a second. I hope you don't mind.

Sometimes when I'm reading a book, I want to stop and say, "That's a great story, but what if we were just talking? You know, just you and me. What if we were sitting across from each other and we were sharing about real life? We had gone beyond the surface stuff about our kids and our weekend plans, and the deeper truths in our hearts were being shared. We were wrestling out how we felt about the future and about our purpose. We were discussing our passions and callings. But then, what if one of us said, 'You know, sometimes I feel like all those big dreams, all those big life issues, are impossible . . . because I am not even sure how I'm supposed to get over this mountain of laundry on my couch.'"

I think it is easy to feel hopeless when we want to think about real heart issues. But really, what would help us today would be an extra set of hands to hold the baby while we run to the bathroom, or for someone to take on the task of finding a match to all those lonely socks. Seriously, can someone just help us with that? Can we find a solution for the daily stuff before we deal with all of the deeper business?

So, I'm going to keep being honest. Maybe even a little more honest than I should be. Can I just stop in the middle of everything and say that I am having a terribly difficult time writing about finding hope in the middle of the messiness of life because I am staring at a living room covered in everyone else's messes as I type? Seriously.

I'm not sure where you imagined I'm sitting as I write these words to you. Or maybe you're not the type of person to think about all of that, but I sure do. I always try to imagine exactly what it looks like from the writer's point of view while she shares what is on her heart. I picture her sitting at some organized desk with color-coded planners and highlighters. Or perhaps she is typing on her laptop, reclining in a deck chair overlooking a lake.

But truthfully, I am sitting on my couch next to a pile of

laundry at nine o'clock at night, with a sink full of dishes and a kids' bathroom that still has wet bath towels on the floor, writing these words to you because this is the only time that I have available to write them. There. That feels better to say! Freedom! (I sang that. You need to know this.)

Seriously. We had pancakes and sausage for dinner (well, my daughter had leftover spaghetti), and the kitchen island is covered in syrup and pasta sauce. The bread bag needs to be closed and put away. The pots soaking in my sink from yesterday need to be washed. And something smells in my refrigerator. This is my view and the aroma, while I write from my messy living room.

I wanted to clean first. Once the kids went to bed, I wanted to get my house in order before I did one more thing, but then I knew that I would be too tired to write. So, I chose you. I chose us. I chose this.

And I'm sitting here trying to think of ways to talk about how we are supposed to find strength or purpose or anything more than desperation in the life around us when everything always seems to revert to a state of chaos . . . while I sit in a house that I swear was clean this morning when I woke up.

And honestly, I have struggled. I have tried to think of just the right story to tell that will paint a picture of how unorganized life can be. I have started and stopped and deleted and rewritten, but you know? Sometimes—actually *oftentimes* — the perfect story doesn't exist. Sometimes, all we have are the real-life, nitty-gritty, can't-get-it-all-done-because-I'm-human-and-that's-okay moments that can be used to help others know that they're not alone right where they are. And what I am starting to realize is that life isn't nearly as pretty as we would like it to be. There isn't the perfect story or the perfect picture or the perfect outfit or the perfect marriage or the perfect family. There are just real people living in real houses with real broken bodies and hearts, all making our way toward healing and grace for our real, messy lives.

So I guess what I'm trying to say is, *this is my story.* This messy old living room and the hours of housework waiting for me are just the right place for me to begin writing these words. And maybe the real-life moment on the other side of this page, where you sit, is exactly where grace can begin to work in your heart as well. Together we will begin to find hope in the reality of everyday life. Because if we're all being honest, things are never quite as put together as we want everyone else to believe (ourselves included). And the sooner we decide that that's okay, the more life we will have to share with those around us.

LIFE WORTH SHARING

About the same time that Jaxton was born a year ago, we started attending a new church. While it is easy to share my life with others on my blog or Facebook page, it is scarier for me to share my heart with new people face to face. Perhaps this goes back to the seventh grade and the way it hurt to feel so alone. Perhaps I have been guarded because I don't want to be rejected. But whatever the root issue is, I ease my way into new friendships slowly, like getting into a pool on a day that's not quite warm enough to swim.

I think the hardest time for me at our new church was when the pastor would ask us to get up and greet one another. I always wanted to sit in my seat and hold my baby, hoping people thought I wasn't being rude, that I just didn't want to disturb my sleeping newborn.

When Jaxton was four months old and babbling, I couldn't quite use that excuse anymore. "Sorry, I can't get up to shake your hand, my baby is sleep—*Shhh,* Jaxton! You're supposed to be sleeping!" Fortunately by then I was starting to feel a little braver when it came to passing around germs. I mean *shaking hands.*

As each week passed, I slowly got to know the other ladies in our church. Casual hellos turned into longer conversations, which turned into invitations to connect outside of church as well. One Sunday, in an attempt to get to know another lady my age in the church, I brought up a popular TV show and suggested that she come over to watch it.

Because that's how you make new friends at thirty. You ask

them if they want to sit around and watch reality TV with you (or at least that's what we do in small-town Oklahoma). She came over, and a few weeks later we invited a few more ladies from the church to join us.

Before I knew it, we had a whole group of ladies coming to my house to find out who was going to get the final rose and become Mrs. Handsome Farmer.

And so, obviously, if there were going to be all of these new people coming to my home, I was going to need three to five weeks to get my house clean enough for this to happen. So I cleaned the living room, the kitchen, the kids' rooms, and the nursery. I scrubbed bathrooms and organized my laundry room. I did ridiculous things like categorize my bookshelf and dust picture frames. And just as everyone was pulling in, I lit a candle, sprayed air freshener, and turned on some worship music to play softly in the background.

Then I opened the door and said, "Hey! Come on in! So sorry that my house is such a wreck." But really I was thinking, *Find some dirt. I dare you!*

Have you ever done something like this? I'm not talking about watching reality TV with a bunch of church ladies. I'm talking about cleaning your home when certain people are coming over and hoping that they believe that it always looks so perfect. Why do you suppose we do this? Why do you think that we hope others believe that our lives don't look lived in?

You know, six months later, when that lady I invited over to watch TV became one of my new best friends, she saw who I really was. As we spent more time together, my house became less and less perfect every time she came by. She got to see the unedited version of my life. She got to see toys on the living room floor and a bathroom that didn't have a hand towel in it and likely had toilet-paper confetti on the floor. She got to see dishes in my sink and clothes on my couch. And now? Well, we just sort of "do life" together. On Saturdays her family comes over and our husbands watch the babies and the football game while we cook and chat in the kitchen.

As a matter of fact, last week after we ate dinner, she stood at my kitchen sink washing not only the dishes from the evening but my dirty dishes that were left over from dinner the night before. Because my messes don't change her opinion of me. It's an honest friendship. We aren't hiding anything. We aren't pretending we have it all together. We are just extending each other the gift of grace and learning from our offering how to receive more grace for ourselves.

So I got to thinking, *Wouldn't life be just so much easier if we were a little more honest with ourselves and others?* If when we presented ourselves to other people we said, "Welcome to my real life. It isn't perfect. Sometimes I fuss at my kids. Sometimes there is something in the refrigerator that makes the entire house stink. There is usually laundry on the couch that needs to be folded, and can you please take this diaper and cram it into the already-full Diaper Genie? . . . So glad you guys could come over and play today!"

What if we just started out being real with people? What if we weren't afraid to be all of who we really are (messes included)? What if we all just decided to stop hiding our messes? I think there would be far more authentic friendships and far fewer closets crammed with real-life opportunities to show ourselves and others grace.

Because, friend, even if you are on top of it when it comes to cleaning and organizing, even if you haven't related to one sentence of my stories about laundry-filled couches, even if you can't stand clutter and your house is always put together, I want you to hear me say this: The messy areas of your life do not tell a story of your failures. Those areas tell the story of your humanity, and they are a continual reminder of your need for a Savior. Friend, those areas are still worth sharing with others.

JUST A MINUTE, JESUS

The truth is, somewhere along the way, we decided that we had to have it all together, all of the time. We decided to set the standard of *"well done"* at "perfection" instead of "the best we can do." I'm not sure what made us do this, but at some point, our hearts chose to believe that if our best wasn't perfect, then we had failed. But it's a lie. We have to stop thinking that anything less than perfect is failure. We have to choose grace for ourselves and our abilities. Because the minute we decide we're going to stop being defined by what we don't get done and instead take pride in what we are able to achieve, grace lets truth win and unnecessary shame gives way to hope.

Because whatever compels us to hide our shortcomings doesn't just compel us to do this with what we present to each other. That sneaky little lie that says we always have to have it all together doesn't just tell us to throw everything in a closet when we hear a neighbor or a guest is coming over. (I can't be the only one who does this.) We often do this with the Lord as well. For some reason, we don't want Him to think that we cannot handle it all on our own.

He's knocking on the door of our hearts, and we are shouting, "Just a minute, Jesus! Hang on! I'm coming!" while we run around and shove all of the issues that are really bothering us into the unvisited corners of our hearts. And then we open the door with a smile, as if to say, "Come on in, Lord. Haven't I handled everything well on my own? Aren't You pleased with how pretty it all looks in here? With how well I've got it all under control?"

And honestly, I think one of the worst things we can do for ourselves and our families is believe that it was ever up to us to clean it all up on our own in the first place. Because the Lord does not only want us when we are pretty or when our lives look organized. He doesn't just want to have a relationship with us when our house is put together and when the socks are matched. He wants to do life with us. He wants to stand with us and encourage our hearts while we wash dishes and while we wrestle with doubts. Because it was never in His plan for us to clean up any mess on our own.

Do you ever feel like maybe there are some messy areas of your heart or your life that you should handle on your own? What do you think keeps you from bringing them before the Lord? Sometimes it's shame. Other times, fear or pride keeps us from taking our struggles to God. But no matter the reason, we need to remember that God would always rather that we bring our hearts before Him, especially when we need help.

Don't Come in Here

It happened midmorning a few months ago. Kolton was in his prekindergarten class at school, and it was just Kadence, six-month-old Jaxton, and me playing on the floor of the living room. Kadence disappeared for a minute, then I heard her in the bathroom. Being nearly four years old, I knew she was able to take care of business on her own. (And praise the Lord! That means I currently only have one child that requires me to wipe his booty. Two down, one to go!) Anyway,

I heard the toilet flush, I heard the water run in the sink, and I didn't think another thing about Kadence's potty break.

A few minutes went by, and she didn't come dancing back into the living room. (Kadence dances everywhere she goes.) I assumed that she had gone down the hall into her bedroom to play quietly, and I kept bouncing Jaxton on my lap, trying to get him to repeat "Momma." I looked up as Kadence popped into the living room and smiled.

"You doin' okay, sweet girl?"

She nodded, while hiding halfway behind the living room chair. Now, for the record, four-year-olds do many questionable things, but hiding intentionally is usually cause for concern.

"Where are your pants?" I asked, as I leaned a little to see what she might be trying to conceal.

"Oh. I just felt like changing them."

"But you didn't put any new ones on . . ."

She giggled a little nervously. "Oh yeah," she said, and then scurried back toward her bedroom, where I assumed she was finding replacement pants. But after a few more minutes of playtime that seemed all too quiet, my mommy-sense started tingling. I stood up, put Jax on my hip, and walked around the corner to investigate. That's when my foot splashed on the dining room floor.

At first, I thought perhaps a drink had spilled. Maybe a water glass or sippy cup . . . but quickly I realized that not only was the dining room floor covered in water, so were the hallway and bathroom floors.

I waded up the Lake-That-Had-Better-Not-Be-Pee to find my daughter sitting on the floor of her bedroom trying to pull on a clean pair of shorts.

"What happened?!" I shouted, not so much angry as concerned that I had no idea a disaster had apparently taken place just a few feet away from where I was sitting, oblivious.

"Um. Well, I put too much toilet paper in da potty, and it oveflowed. Da potty has cracks in da sides of it. Did you know dat, Mommy? Da water came out da sides of it. It just kept coming. Even wif da wid shut. I fell too. I was trying to clean it up, and I fell down in it." (Thus the missing pants.)

I stood there, taking in the moment. The bathroom was flooded, the hallway was flooded, and there were tiny wet footprints and drips leading to her bedroom where, underneath a tower of her favorite storybooks and toys, she had attempted to hide towels that she had used to soak up some of the mess. "Why didn't you tell me?" I asked, heartbroken at the thought of her struggling without me.

"Because I was afwaid."

I had no idea where to begin, but I was sad that my little girl had hidden her problem from me instead of running to get my help at the first sign of trouble. You know, I bet she thought she was golden when she shut the lid on the potty.

But just like us, she can't always put a lid on her mess and expect to contain it.

Sometimes messes are bigger than we are. But who likes to admit that? We're doing all we know to do to handle the situations that are less than ideal in our lives, and the last thing we think to do is go to the One who can help us. We are so busy trying to clean it all up on our own, saying, "Just don't be mad, God. I got this. It's my fault. I can clean this up. I can make this right." But like my daughter, we are hiding our messes when we should be seeking our Father. And instead of saying, "I've got this. Don't come in here," we should be saying, "My Lord, can You help me? Can You just come close? Can You bend down low and wipe away the grime and the sticky places in my heart that remind me of my failure?"

And He does. Every single time, He does.

Because messes don't bother Jesus. Never have. Never will.

I Am Martha

In Scripture, we read about Jesus coming to visit the home of two sisters, Mary and Martha:

> As Jesus and his disciples were on their way, he came to
> a village where a woman named Martha opened her
> home to him. She had a sister called Mary, who sat at

the Lord's feet listening to what he said. But Martha was
distracted by all the preparations that had to be made.
She came to him and asked, "Lord, don't you care that
my sister has left me to do the work by myself? Tell her
to help me!"

"Martha, Martha," the Lord answered, "you are
worried and upset about many things, but few things
are needed—or indeed only one. Mary has chosen what
is better, and it will not be taken away from her."[11]

I used to read this passage and think, *I am so glad that I'm
not like Martha. I am so glad that if Jesus were sitting in my
living room I would not be silly enough to think that I should
be anywhere other than in the living room sitting right next to
Him.*

One day, when Kadence was two, I was waist deep in cha-
otic life and the stresses of what was on the calendar for the rest
of the week. I was doing my best to get dinner on the table and
get a head start on my to-do list when my daughter brought me
her pink ballerina dress and asked me to put it on her. At the
time, it seemed like one more thing that I was going to have to
clean up when she was done with it, but I put it on her and went
back to unloading the groceries from the bags on the counter. I
was just about done when I looked up and saw this precious
two-year-old standing in our living room with a mess all around

her, dancing and swaying to the worship music playing on my phone.

And as I watched her dance, completely caught up in this act of grace, I realized that sometimes being Martha doesn't look like choosing something else over Jesus. It simply looks like forgetting that He is always in the room. I think Jesus was onto something when He told Martha that she worried about many things but only one thing was really needed. He knew that since the beginning of time, women have been trying to clean up their own messes, and He has to remind them that only Jesus can do that. Because the truth is, there is no beauty in our mess until we expose it to our Maker, and when Jesus looks at dirt, He always sees destiny.

A Little Dirt Work

I was talking to my friend one afternoon over the phone. I knew that she had plenty on her plate, and she was sharing about a few different situations she was currently sorting out. We decided together that we would simply continue to bring it all before the Lord in prayer and trust His able hands to take care of it all. And she said, "Becky, I just feel like I'm always asking God to fix everything. I wonder if sometimes He gets tired of hearing me ask." And I reminded her, "God is in the business of fixing messes. Since Adam and Eve, God has been putting back together what was broken. It's in His very nature."

She agreed with me, but I kept thinking about this long after we got off the phone. See, what the Lord showed me is that He's not afraid to step into the moments where we absolutely need Him the most. The moments where we feel covered by chaos. He's not afraid to wipe down the things that bury our hearts in earth. Because the Word of God says that when God made Adam, He reached into the dirt and, out of the clay, formed a man.[12] He breathed life into that mess of earth and only then did man come alive. Because God doesn't see things as they are but as He calls them to be. And that means just like He reached into the mud and pulled out a man, Jesus reaches into our messes and pulls out miracles over and over again.

God's best work happens when His hands get a hold of dirt, but He will never have a chance to show us what He is capable of doing with our shortcomings if we do our best to keep our real-life struggles hidden.

Look, I know that there are moments in your day when you feel overwhelmed too. I know that there are moments where you are on your hands and knees, cleaning up and sorting through and fighting the never-ending battle between order and chaos. I know that there are days when, at the end of them, not even a hot shower could wash away the stresses that seem to soil the fabric of your heart.

But friend, in those moments, I want you to remember that Jesus is there with you, and I want you to see Him draw close and pull off the heavy garment of your day. I want you to imagine Him wiping away the worries and the cares and all of the moments when you felt like you just wanted to scream. See Him take the guilt and the frustration and the feelings of inadequacy. And then in a beautiful exchange, as you stand there with your heart exposed like the fresh skin under an old wound, see Him replace all of the heaviness with hope. A hope that fits you perfectly. A hope that is tailor-made for every moment you have walked through and every moment you will face up ahead. A hope that will still be there underneath it all tomorrow, no matter what. Because it is a hope that is forever unfolding—and it never stops short of being all that we need.

Let's Talk

I have this junk drawer in my house that just keeps accumulating more stuff. It started out as the drawer in my kitchen that holds our potato masher and the egg separator and those little spiky handles that you push into the ends of corncobs that make them easier to eat.

Basically, it was full of all the stuff that I didn't use very often but didn't necessarily want to get rid of. But because of where the drawer sits in my kitchen, and because my husband is forever asking me if I know where he could find a pen, I decided to add a pen to that drawer. Unfortunately, that pen made me feel like other things could live in that drawer as well. LEGOs and Barbie shoes that I found on the floor, coins, ChapStick, spare batteries, gum, and a purple marker all call that drawer home as well. It was just easier to tuck it all away than find a more appropriate place for everything.

You know, our hearts can act a lot like our junk drawers— full of things that are easier to think about later. And before we know it, we've got all of these things that we feel responsible for dealing with on our own, and we don't even know where to begin to sort through it all.

Are there things tucked into the corners of your heart where you hope no one will look? Are there issues or hurts or problems that you are uneasy about letting others discover? Why do you think you keep these things to yourself? Do you feel responsible to take care of it? Maybe you feel that you got yourself into the situation and you really don't want to involve God if you don't have to. Or perhaps you feel that God's just not interested in helping you, for whatever reason.

What areas can you invite God to take hold of and sort through and clean up with you?

Now, I want you to try this: Ask the Lord to help you. Tell the Lord that you're done keeping things to yourself, and imagine that door to your heart opening wider as the Lord walks in and sets things right again.

Let's Pray

Father, I thank You for seeing worth in this dirt. I thank You for loving us despite our messes. I thank You for taking all of the things about us that don't seem so put together and finding value in them. Set things in order, Lord. We give You all of ourselves—and that includes the not-so-pretty parts, because we believe that in Your hands even our messes can be used to bring You glory. In Jesus's name we pray, amen.

Let's Hope

I am not a mess. I am a miracle. God sees value in me. God wants to help me, and I will let Him.

7

Don't Run Her Race

HAVE GRACE FOR WHO YOU ARE

Five years ago, when Kolton was just a few weeks old, Jared and I decided that we would take our new baby with us and go to IHOP for breakfast. Well, I guess it was really more like lunch. I had already learned in the first few days of motherhood that if it takes you an hour to get ready in the morning before you have children, then once a baby arrives, it will take like six to seven months to get out the door. Give or take.

I had packed the diaper bag that morning including all of the essentials—diapers, wipes, extra pacifiers, clothing, burp rags, diaper rash paste, nipple ointment since I was nursing, a thermometer, a bulb syringe, and a toy (so that he could work on his three-week-old fine-motor skills). Basically, I just brought the entire nursery. I have learned since then that when you're breastfeeding, all you really need is your body and a diaper and some wipes. The rest is optional.

This is the difference between baby one and baby three, but I digress.

After we loaded everything into the car (which took something like fifteen minutes and a dozen trips), I looked at the clock and realized that Kolton would be ready to nurse just as the food was being served. And I panicked a little.

Don't get me wrong, I knew before I even became a momma that I would stand my ground when it came to nursing my baby in public. I mean, I was *not* going to be one of those mothers who was confined to the bathroom stall, surrounded by flushing toilets, while she nursed her sweet baby. Not cool. I had already decided that no matter where we were when Kolton was hungry, I was going to break out my nursing cover and feed him—and that's all there was to it. Until, of course, we arrived at IHOP for breakfast . . . I mean lunch.

It was one of our first outings as a family of three. I was tense, and looking back I'm not quite sure why. I really didn't have a reason to be, but there I was, waiting for a meltdown, nervously ordering my eggs and bacon, constantly peeking into the baby carrier sitting next to me in the booth.

Spoiler alert. This ends badly.

I think I was finally settling into the idea that we were

going to survive the trip, when that classic piercing new-baby cry came from under the car-seat cover.

"He's hungry," I whispered to Jared, who was sitting on the other side of the booth. "What do I do?"

Now, my husband, like most men, is a problem solver, and so it wasn't too hard for him to answer, "Um. Feed him?"

"Here?!" I asked, a little shocked that he would even suggest something so audacious. "There are children and elderly people just trying to eat their brunch!" I reminded him in a stern whisper. My eyes darted around the room. "No one wants to see me nurse while they eat pancakes."

"Okay. So, use your cover," Jared suggested.

I had forgotten how brave I was going to be. Or how firm I would be concerning what was best for my baby and my family, whatever society's judgmental opinions might be. But you know, right there in the middle of IHOP, society didn't seem like some distant hypothetical group. Society seemed like the folks in the next booth eating French toast and getting their coffee refilled.

"Okay, I'm going to do this, but I need the nursing cover and the blanket from the bag." I was going to nurse my baby right there at the table. I wouldn't draw any attention. I would be the definition of discreet.

I need to mention that Kolton was wailing at this point. He

didn't do hungry well. He did hungry loud. And his loud hungry drew plenty of attention. There was no secrecy about anything happening at our table. Everyone was looking. But before I could pick up the baby and stop his crying, I needed to tent myself. Yes, I said *tent*.

I had one nursing cover going one way and another nursing cover going another way, and I threw on a blanket on top of those for good measure.

"There. Now no one can see anything!"

I'm sure Jared was thinking, *Oh, you're something to see all right.*

I got Kolton out of his car seat, put him under the tent, and attempted to maneuver everything just right, while completely blind to what was happening. It was difficult to say the least. And let me just say that for someone who was aiming for discretion, I was doing an awfully good job of putting on quite the show.

Nothing to see here, folks, I thought. *Nooooothing worth watching is happening at this table.*

And then it happened . . . right as the kind, unassuming waitress brought us our water.

A long, loud, up-the-back, down-the-legs, on-everyone-and-everything blowout. Remember the big BP oil spill in the Gulf of Mexico that sent nearly 210 million gallons of oil into the water and required years of cleanup? This diaper was like that.

I just sat there. Frozen.

Jared was sitting across from me, asking if he should choose bacon or sausage, and I'm looking at him like there is an asteroid headed for the restaurant—just over his shoulder.

"Jared! Jared! It's everywhere."

"What's everywhere?"

"Poop! Kolton pooped everywhere!"

My sweet husband, always the voice of reason, protested, "It can't be that bad."

I thought maybe he was right. Perhaps under my inconspicuous tent there was less of a disaster than I had originally believed. I lifted the bottom of the nursing covers so my husband could have a good view of what horrors had taken place.

His face said it all. He had no words.

"What do I do?!?"

He just shook his head with his mouth half-open, like he wanted to say something but couldn't. If the back of the booth hadn't been holding him firmly in place, I'm certain he would have backed away slowly while shielding his eyes.

"Don't just look at me! What DO I *DO*?" I asked again.

He still had no words. Seriously, friend, I am not sure what I was worried about on my way into the restaurant when I was anxious about our breakfast outing. But this? This was much worse. This is one of those moments that you cannot fully recover from. It's one of those moments that you point back to every time you change another diaper and say, "At least it wasn't like that one time Kolton pooped at IHOP."

I slid out of the booth and started to wander. I think I was heading toward the bathroom.

And that's when that intuitive parenting thing kicked in.

How much easier would it be to just open the back hatch of our SUV and change the baby on the clean, flat surface of the cargo area? *Good idea, Becky,* I thought.

I was totally winning at this whole mommy thing.

But as I stepped outside, I realized it was still January and it was still cold, and standing outside to change the baby would be miserable. So I just crawled up into the back cargo area with Kolton, then closed the hatch behind us.

In the quiet confinement of the back of our vehicle, I changed the baby, cleaned us both, and prepared to step back into the restaurant. It was about that time that I realized those smarty-pants designers of the Chevrolet TrailBlazer did not include a door latch on the inside of the cargo space (because people don't go back there . . . obviously). I would have to crawl over the back row of seats to get out. The thing was, I could not crawl over and carry my newborn at the same time. It just wasn't possible.

So, I laid Kolton down on the floor of the cargo space, climbed over the seats by myself, went out the door, around to the back, opened the hatch, and picked up my newborn.

But as I picked up the baby and closed the back hatch, I realized that about a dozen people had come out of the restaurant just as I was retrieving Kolton.

Their faces said it all! They thought that I had driven to IHOP with my newborn just rolling around in the cargo space. These uninformed onlookers had no idea what had taken place earlier. They didn't know my story or the crazy events that had brought me to that cold parking lot on that January day. I seriously wanted to explain. "Wait! This is *not* what it looks like." But there was no time. They all gave me a quick side-eye before they hurried on their way to share a great story about the lady who didn't have a proper car seat. I bet they still tell that story every chance they get: "So then, she just pops the back hatch and gets out her baby! No, I'm serious, Janet. It was the craziest thing."

The problem is, they had seen everything about that moment, but they hadn't seen what led up to it. They didn't know the whole story, and they certainly didn't know me.

Just a Part of Her Story

Have you ever had something like that happen to you? A moment while running errands or at the park when you were certain that others made assumptions about you and your child that just weren't accurate? You wanted to say something like, "I promise she doesn't always act this way." Or, "We missed our nap, so we're extra cranky this afternoon." Or maybe you didn't want to say anything at all. You just wanted to run and hide.

Friend, that day in the IHOP parking lot, I learned that just because we see part of someone's story does not mean we know all there is to tell. The people that we encounter every day have been walking a long road before they ever happened to cross our paths. The most unfortunate thing we can do is assume we know them because of one fleeting moment in the chronicles of their life story.

We do that though, don't we? We see that other mom in the grocery store and she doesn't seem to have any grace left for her kids. We wonder if she is always that stern. We see that her kids are crying, we see a mom who is yelling, and we decide that surely there are things that this mean momma could have done to prevent a catastrophe at the checkout.

But in that moment, we have fallen victim to believing only our own senses. We have fallen victim to the lie that what we have seen is all there is to know. When in reality, we only saw a fraction of her day, just one sentence of her story. We saw a problem that could have been solved differently instead of a woman who needed compassion. And deep down, I think we know that.

I think we know that we are too quick to make rash assumptions of each other. So why do we do it? I wonder sometimes if we aren't really just a little bit afraid to be like that other mom. She looks like she's doing a terrible job, so if I relate to her, then what does that say about me?

We size her up, trying to figure out what separates us from her, hopeful that we can find something that will assure us that we won't ever have a similar experience at the checkout counter, or park or mall.

The truth is, we are all more alike than we realize. Because those other mommas we run into have stories just like we do — we just don't get to see them. We don't see that her husband is working out of town, her boss just called and moved up an important deadline, the baby is running a fever, and no one in the house got a good night's sleep. We don't see her cry her way to the store, or cry her way home. We don't see all of the moments of love that she pours out endlessly on those sweet babies, the books she reads them at bedtime, or how she goes in and checks on her kids after they have fallen asleep . . . just like we do every night. We don't see a woman who is just like us — in need of grace.

There are billions of other parents on this planet who are all walking different roads, with one common theme: we are all doing the very best that we can. What if we stopped looking for ways that we are different and started looking for ways to encourage and help each other? What if we made the point to look at one another with eyes that don't try to separate but that see the places where we might connect?

We are all women finding our way toward grace, loved by the Father, daughters of the King, and sisters in this often overwhelming world of motherhood. And you know what? No one understands like other mommas how hard it is to be a mom.

So my challenge is simple. The next time you go out and come across another mom, don't just see her moment. Try to really see her. Try to remember that you are on the same team.

Against the Wall

It's not always the failures of others that we use as a tool to measure our own self-worth. Sometimes, we're guilty of comparing ourselves to others' successes as well.

I measure my babies on the back wall in my bathroom. They love for me to put their little feetsies up against the trim board, hold their arms by their sides, and take my special marker to make a dot just above their heads to show them how much they have grown. My son has his own set of notches, and my daughter has another. Baby Jaxton isn't quite big enough to have his own marks yet, but soon he will.

Each of my children is different. Not only are they separated by age, but they are each unique individuals on their own growth tracks. When I finish measuring Kadence, I don't compare her marks to Kolton's and say, "Well, you still come up short. Too bad you will never catch him."

That would be ridiculous. Instead, each child focuses on his or her own growth. They look at where they were and how far they have come. And we cheer each time.

A few years ago, I watched this video on Facebook of my friend's son reading ... at eighteen months. I must have watched that video a dozen times, looking for some sort of trick that was being played. Was someone off camera mouthing the words to him? It couldn't be real, because that would mean that my own son could ... no ... *should* be reading too. Had I failed him? Would he ever catch up? How had he fallen so far behind developmentally?

I found myself considering all of the wonderful things that my son was able to do. I wondered if this other little boy would measure up to all of my son's impressive skills. For some reason, I felt as if I had to make this other little boy less than amazing so that my son could be equal. What is that? Why do we do that? It wasn't a healthy way to think, but I realize that we do this when it comes to comparing ourselves to other women also.

Pinterest, Facebook, and Instagram help us so much. They give us great ideas and inspire us. But they are also like looking at another woman's growth marks on the wall and comparing our abilities to hers. We can easily fall victim to the lie that we aren't good enough when we use another woman's successes to measure our own. Friend, there is something very freeing about realizing that you have been guilty of measuring yourself against others. There is something even more freeing about stepping away from the wall and letting your worth be found in who God says you are.

FACING THE GIANTS

So I have friends who run marathons. Do you have any friends who do that? Are you a runner? I am not. I buy running shoes and clothes and sometimes those sporty headbands to keep my hair out of my face when I am not running, but that is about as far as I get. I would love to be a runner. Maybe someday I will say that I am, but for now, as I type these words to you, running is not on the list of activities that I enjoy—even though I just bought a super cute pair of black-and-white running shoes a few months ago. I wore them to pick up my daughter from pre-K. I secretly hoped that the other mommas thought that I perhaps had gotten in a quick jog that morning. I did not.

Do you know who probably did? My friend Randi. She is a real runner—and not in a "Hey, everyone is a runner these days" sort of way. Randi runs marathons—frequently—and often finishes in the top 10 percent, if not first. Oh, and as if running weren't enough, Randi also competes in those extreme challenges where the contestants climb walls, crawl through mud, run with five-gallon buckets of sand, and jump over fire. The last time I checked, she was ranked in the top ten women in the world who compete in extreme challenges. I told you Randi is awesome.

After one of her races, Randi posted a photo on social media of herself looking like a character in a movie, covered in grime, leaping over fire. I just so happened to be sitting on my couch eating another handful of those fudge-covered Oreo cookies when I saw her picture. I mumbled to myself through another cookie bite, "How'd she even get up that high?" But I already knew the answer. Randi can jump over fire and not get burned because of each moment that took place before she came to the moment where she had to face that obstacle. Each step that Randi took was readying her body to walk (or run) every step that would follow. Randi trained. She prepared. She conditioned herself to be able to conquer it. When I was driving into town to go to the store with my little kids, she was running there with her jogging stroller.

I could try to take on the same obstacles, but I would fail. Not because I am a failure, but because Randi and I are running different races. And as much as I might wish I were more like Randi, the truth is, I'm not prepared to face her giants. And that's okay.

TAKE OFF WHAT SLOWS YOU DOWN

In Scripture, there is a story of a young man named David who worked in his father's fields, taking care of sheep. His brothers were men of war, but David, being one of the youngest brothers, stayed behind and tended to the sheep. It might sound much less exciting than the battlefield, but Scripture says that David had some of his own victories while in the fields. David, recounting his own story, said, "When a lion or a bear came and carried off a sheep from the flock, I went after it, struck it and rescued the sheep from its mouth. When it turned on me, I seized it by its hair, struck it and killed it."[13]

What did I do today? Oh, just grabbed a lion by its beard and took a sheep from its mouth. No big deal . . .

Once, David went to visit his brothers at war, and when he arrived, he found a warrior from the opposing army taunting his people. Everyone was afraid of this giant man named Goliath. And every day, Goliath would ask for someone to fight him. No one was brave enough to answer the challenge. Of all the Israelites, only young David wasn't afraid of him.

Hearing this, King Saul sent for David. He listened to this young man's heart, yet when David offered to go up against Goliath, Saul replied, "You are not able to go out against this Philistine and fight him; you are only a young man, and he has been a warrior from his youth." But David convinced the king to let him try.

> Then Saul dressed David in his own tunic. He put a coat of armor on him and a bronze helmet on his head. David fastened on his sword over the tunic and tried walking around, because he was not used to them.
>
> "I cannot go in these," he said to Saul, "because I am not used to them." So he took them off. Then he took his staff in his hand, chose five smooth stones from the stream, put them in the pouch of his shepherd's bag and, with his sling in his hand, approached the Philistine.[14]

And with just a slingshot and a stone, David defeated the giant.

Do you know what I love about David? I love that he was smart enough to recognize that Saul's armor would only slow him down. David realized that the armor wasn't made for him, wouldn't fit him, and would only hinder his ability to fight.

Do you know what else I love about David? Scripture says that he took off the armor and picked up his staff—the same staff that he had used while tending the sheep. You know, I heard it preached once by my favorite pastor (my dad) that the staff of a man in those days wasn't just used for walking. It told the story of his life—especially a shepherd's staff. Men would make a notch or a mark in the staff for each significant event in their lives, and David's staff probably had marks from when he killed the lion and the bear.

I'd like to imagine that as David took off Saul's armor and picked up his staff, he was reminding himself of exactly who he was. He took off Saul and picked up David and declared that who he was and who God was in him were enough to face the giant.

There are times when I look around and see other women and moms who seem to have it all together. They love their husbands and their families well. They are punctual, practical, polished, and poised, and I wonder what it would be like to be them. But if I take away anything from the story of David and Goliath, it shouldn't just be that little guys can take on a giant and win. What I should learn from David is that the only way you can defeat your giant is if you face it with what you've learned in the fields with the sheep.

Everything you have been through has been preparing you to be *this* momma to *these* kids and *this* wife to *this* husband. God has been shaping your heart and conditioning your spirit so that you are fully equipped to handle everything about this moment in your life. And, Momma, the only way we will find true acceptance of ourselves will be when we decide that we aren't going to try to be anyone else.

❧ Let's Talk

I wrote a story on my blog about a time when I went to the grocery store and got the evil eye from a lady in the frozen-food section. Granted, I had been running through the store with a cart full of kids, and I was singing loudly and making quite the scene, but when I looked up as I grabbed my take-and-bake pizza, she was glaring at me. I felt completely judged. I felt small. I felt like I owed her an explanation for my appearance and behavior and, well, for my entire life. But as I recounted the story, I realized that I was frustrated about being judged, when really I had done the same thing to her. Perhaps she had had a long day. Perhaps she wasn't glaring—perhaps she had a headache and was just intently curious (no, she was absolutely glaring, but I'm giving her grace).

The truth is, I didn't know any more of her story than she knew of mine, but neither of us wanted to feel judged.

Looking back, was there ever a time when you felt misjudged? What happened? Were you able to correct the other person's opinion of you? How did that make you feel?

It can be so easy to fall victim to the lie that if we just could be a little more like another woman that we admire, our lives would be __________ [easier? better? more fulfilled?]. But the truth is, the only way to find true acceptance of who we are and true peace in our purpose is to seek the presence of the Lord. In Him alone, our identities can truly be found. What are some things that set you apart? that make you, well, you?

Let's Pray

So, Lord? I thank You for every moment that led us here today—my typing words on a keyboard, and my friend holding them in her hands and reading them. I thank You for seeing each of us. I thank You for knowing each of us. And I thank You for loving each of us. Help us to remember what You say about us. Help us to remember that You say we are more than enough through Christ Jesus. Help us to remember that You say we can face anything up ahead, not just because You will meet us there but because You have equipped us in the moments that are leading up to it. Soften our hearts to receive Your grace. Soften our hearts to hear only Your Truth. In Jesus's name we pray, amen.

❧ Let's Hope

I don't have to be jealous or envious or defensive. I will choose grace for others and for myself. We are both enough.

8

Outside the Box

GOD STILL PERFORMS MIRACLES

 still don't like dark confined spaces, and if I'm honest, my dislike began one night when I was five. It was the night of our church carnival. There were rides and games, and the coordinators had constructed a huge maze using old over-sized cardboard boxes. The maze started on one end of the gymnasium and stretched across the floor, with dead ends and little places to pop up and look out along the way. To this day, I would love to make one of those for my kids. Doesn't it sound like fun? Of course, I have come to realize that our expectations about how we will feel about something and the way we actually feel once the moment arrives are often two completely different things.

I had been there earlier in the day when the maze was being

constructed. Hours before the carnival began, I had played in the small sections of it, using the taller boxes as my own personal fort. I guess that is how it works for the pastor's kid sometimes. We get to enjoy some of the behind-the-scenes stuff like the construction of carnival games. But playing in the pieces of the maze in the afternoon wasn't anything like crawling into the fully formed tunnel later that night. And I wasn't prepared for the stark difference.

I stood in line for what seemed like forever, watching as the kids in front of me dropped down onto their hands and knees and crawled into the tunnel's dark mouth. Squeals of laughter echoed down the shadowy passages and escaped in the bright fluorescent lights. I couldn't wait to join them. After a few minutes, two sweaty-looking figures popped out of the other end of the maze, and I got the go-ahead to enter.

I bent down and scurried into the madness. I'm not sure what I had imagined, but it was darker than I thought it would be. The maze makers had cut star-shaped holes in the tops of the boxes, but they didn't let in much light (or let out the stuffy cardboard smell). No matter how much I strained, I could only see just about a foot in front of me. I realized quickly that the only way to move forward would be to feel my way in the dark.

Have you ever been in seasons of life that feel like that? You were sure that you were prepared for something, only to get into it and realize that it was not exactly as you imagined that it would be at all? You had glimpses of what it might be like before it was your turn, but once you were committed to it, once you were fully in it, you understood that it wasn't going to be like the playtime earlier?

I have to be honest. Aside from the carnival maze, I have felt that way at least twice in my life. The first was after I became a wife. And the second after I became a momma. I guess I just had all these unrealistic expectations of what life might be like as a momma. I am not sure how I formed these opinions, since I had never been around anyone else's baby before my own. Truthfully, the only time that I had ever been responsible for children was when my husband and I were asked to watch our niece and nephew one night. Their parents called us last minute, and Jared and I rushed over to take the kids to McDonald's . . . at 9:30 p.m. But after that brief experience, I remember thinking I could totally handle this motherhood thing. Because clearly I knew what I was doing. Except it was the equivalent of playing in the deconstructed boxes when I was five. My thoughts of what motherhood would be like were nowhere close to what it actually felt like when I became a momma . . . and was feeling my way along in the dark.

I remember coming to my first dead end that night in the gym. The girl in front of me said calmly, "Oh, we have to turn around," then pushed past me and continued on her way. I followed her lead until, suddenly, I couldn't make out the backs of hite sneakers in front of me anymore. She was gone, and I was all alone.

Suddenly, the box felt very small and very dark and very forever. My heart was pounding in my ears, my warm breath heating up the confined space. And fear began to whisper: *"You're going to be stuck in this box forever. No one even knows you are in here. You can try to find your way out, but it will be pointless. You're just going to run into another dead end. You are lost, and you are trapped."*

I was five, and so I believed the fear. I sat down, pulled my knees to my chest, and started to cry. I wish I could say that I was brave. I wish I could say that I cried for a minute, then rallied and crawled my way out of the darkness. But the truth is, I sat down and waited. I couldn't tell you how long I sat there crying. I just know it felt like an eternity. I felt hopeless.

I'm Stuck Here

Friend, before we go on, let me just say that I know there are some really overwhelming situations in life. Situations that make everything else seem small and insignificant. I don't know what you're going through or what you have already been through, but I want to speak just a few words of truth to this anxious area. You're not stuck. You will come out of this, because God's not going to leave you in the dark.

The other day I found an old journal entry from shortly after I became a momma. Kolton wasn't even three months old, but I had already quit my job and lost touch with many of my friends. Outside of work, I hadn't had the chance to make new friends. If you couple this with the fact that I was the first in my group of friends to get married or have a baby, it was a lonely start to motherhood. But in those short three months, my journal revealed an interesting fact. I had already experienced something I think many mommas often feel.

> I am invisible. There is still a me down in here some-
> where. A me who is more than a mommy and a wife. A
> me that is funny and happy and sure. I feel so insecure
> about everything—about who I am as a mom. About
> who I am as a wife. And I don't even have anyone to tell.
> I need help. I need help remembering who I was, and
> who I am. I need someone to find me here, but no one
> even knows that I'm stuck in this place.

Isn't it interesting that the fears I had as a new mom were the same fears I had as a child? That the feelings of being stuck and alone and unseen came over my heart again decades later? I believe the reason is simple: The Enemy of our hearts doesn't have any new tricks. He speaks the same lies over and over again to the hearts of women to try to keep us wrapped up in fear — to keep us from living in the fullness of what God has for us.

Satan's unrelenting words tell us, *"It's always going to be this way. It's always going to be this hard or difficult. It's always going to be this overwhelming, and there's no end in sight."* But the voice of Truth cannot be silenced. The voice of Truth resounds deep throughout our hearts. It echoes off the walls of the place within us created solely for inhabitation of the King. God declares, *"But I am the miracle maker. And I can change everything in an instant."*

Sometimes, all it takes is telling someone how we feel. And that is exactly what I did as I called out from the dark confinement of the maze.

The walls felt like they were closing in . . . I couldn't catch my breath. I started to cry harder. Louder. And I decided that I couldn't wait for someone to find me. I needed to let someone know I was trapped. I began to beat on the side of the box. "Daddy! Mooooommmma! I want out! Help! Get me out of here!

"Moooommma!"

SAY "MOMMA"

Jaxton was six months old the first time that he said "Dada," and it was a complete fluke. Well, unless you ask Jared, and then that baby knew exactly what he was saying. I denied it because Jax is likely my last baby, and his first word is not supposed to be "Dada." It is supposed to be "Momma," obviously. So I began to really up my game when it came to teaching Jaxton how to say my name.

I accentuated the letter *m* in every word. When I got him out of his crib each day, I would say, "Good mmmmmmmmorning, Jaxton!" Or if I was feeding him food in his highchair, I would ask him if he would like some "mmmmmmmmore." I did this so often that Kadence started calling me "Mmmmm-Momma" when speaking to Jaxton.

"Jaxton, quit trying to get my toys! Go see Mmmmm-Momma!"

It was late one night a few weeks later when Jaxton couldn't settle down for bed. It was likely because he had fallen asleep around 5 p.m., taking one of those bedtime-busting naps. (In all of motherhood, nothing is more frustrating than potty training and a baby that falls asleep at dinnertime.) But there we were, wide awake at midnight, paying the consequences of a late afternoon nap.

Since Jaxton was not interested in sleep or anything to do with sleep, we played on my bed quietly, while the rest of the world was still around us.

We were playing peekaboo, patty-cake, and keep-mommy-awake-because-she-had-a-long-day-and-didn't-get-a-nap, when all of a sudden, baby Jax said, "Mmmmaaaa!" I sat straight up and shouted, "Did you say, 'Momma'?"

I was so happy that I cried. (And for the record, he cried too . . . but mostly because in my excitement I had shouted and scared him.) A lovely memory.

But I couldn't believe it. I had waited so long to hear him say my name, and when he finally did, I wanted to make a promise to him right then that every time he said Momma, it would be just as meaningful as it was the first time.

You know, that word *Momma* is powerful. It just might be one of the most powerful words in the entire world. Because when our children call to us, we respond. Every single time.

The word *Momma* has sent women running across dark houses in the middle of the night to get to a crying baby. It has sent women running across playgrounds to reach children who have fallen. It has inspired women to run into burning buildings to save their babies. And it causes you and me to help our children in every way that we can . . . just because they say that word.

You know, I bet that you run to your kids when they call out to you in the night, and I bet I know why. It's not because they call out nicely, or because they say the right words. It's not because they remind you that they are your kids and it is your job to take care of them. They don't have to beg or plead or convince. They simply have to call out your name.

Momma! And you show up just because you love them. Every single time. You scoop up your little boy who had a bad dream, or you comfort your little girl who needs a hug. You feed a hungry baby who is standing in his crib waiting for you to hold him. Or just let your presence push away fear. No matter how tired you are, no matter how many times they call you, no matter what they need—they say your name, and you show up.

What makes us think that our heavenly Father would be any different?

I think sometimes we convince ourselves that we need to say all of the right words, or we feel like we need to give Him a list of the reasons why He should help. Can you imagine how ridiculous that would be with our own kids?

God doesn't require us to do that either. He doesn't respond to us because of anything we do or don't do. He doesn't come because of anything we are or aren't. He doesn't answer because we do or do not deserve it.

God responds when we call because He *loves* us. Just because He loves us. And He runs to us every single time. Just because you say His name. And my own dad illustrated this the night he came to rescue me from the maze.

A Rescue

I was crying so hard that I could barely hear the muffled voices of my parents coming from the other side of the cardboard walls.

"Becky! You're okay! We'll get you out! Just a second, sweetheart."

A few other kids who had already been through the tunnel came in to get me. "We can show you how to get out of here. We can show you the way." But I was paralyzed with fear. I couldn't move. I didn't want to know the way out. I didn't want to be led out. I just wanted to *be* out.

Ever been there? Ever been stuck in a situation and others keep offering advice, like telling you that if you do what they did, then you could be free too? You know, sometimes people have the best intentions, but we don't want to try what worked for them. We want them to simply stay with us and yell out to God, to pray until He shows up and makes a way.

The next thing I remember was hearing the knife cut through the cardboard. First one line, then another, and then the side of the box opened up like a door. The bright gym lights and cool air washed over me as I was lifted out of the maze. My dad held me tight to his chest and whispered, "I've got you. You're safe. It's okay." And I cried harder than ever. Tears of relief poured down my face. I was safe. I was free. My daddy had me.

Some days, I feel just like that little girl again. I have gone into seasons knowing that God knows exactly where I am. Knowing that I'm not unreachable. Knowing that there will likely be a few dead ends along the way. And yet, I get scared. I feel lost and alone. And worst of all, I feel trapped by difficult circumstances that seem to have no solution. I just want a miracle.

Maybe you have felt the same way. Like you're on your hands and knees, feeling your way along in the dark. The circumstances that surround the situation are not pleasant. As a matter of fact, they might be uncomfortable. But the more you look around, wondering if things could ever possibly get better, the more convinced you become that they will never change.

The truth is, in an instant God can reach into our situation and pull us out, give us hope, and set our feet on new ground. The truth is, there is no place that you can go that is outside of God's ability to reach you. There is no darkness that cannot be overcome by His light. And even though He is constantly telling your heart that He knows the way, that He can see the way out, He is the type of Father who says that when you don't think you can go any farther, He will pierce the problem and create a way where there seems to be no way. He will reach into your situation and pull you out and into the safety of His arms, just because He loves you. This is what I needed to remind myself about a year ago, right after Jaxton was born.

STORMS SCARIER THAN THESE

Jaxton was two days old and sleeping downstairs in the Neonatal Intensive Care Unit of the hospital. I had been bumped up from the fourth floor that housed labor and delivery and the NICU, and I was now a patient of the ninth floor. This did not make me special. It wasn't like winning a prize. As a matter of fact, the charge nurse apologized that they had to move me, but they needed my bed for another momma.

In that hospital, the babies are allowed to room in with their mommies instead of going to a nursery. The moms have a special bracelet, and the babies have a matching bracelet. They serve as security bands and should the baby go past the doors on the fourth floor, the alarm will sound and the hospital will go on lockdown.

When the fourth floor filled up that August weekend, the nurses had to decide what they would do. They couldn't send a mom with a baby rooming in to another floor that was unsecured.

But me? Well, I didn't have a baby in my room. My baby was in the NICU, so I was the one who could safely move up to the ninth floor.

I think I was one of the most difficult patients that the ninth floor has ever cared for. Most of the patients weren't having Chinese takeout delivered to the nurses' station for a patient named "Becky," and most patients didn't have to have notes left for them saying they needed to have their vitals checked the next time they were actually in the room.

I spent most of my time on the fourth floor NICU with my baby because I wasn't concerned about myself. As a matter of fact, I had forgotten almost completely that I was a patient too . . . which is why I didn't pay much attention when the nurse mentioned my low heart rate during one of the rounds where she had actually caught me in my room. She didn't seem too concerned about it, and so I wasn't either. I had plenty of other things to worry about.

Except I wish that I had paid a little more attention. I wish that I had asked more questions about my own health.

Our arrival home was just what I wanted it to be. The two older kids were thrilled to welcome their baby brother. They took turns holding him and taking pictures with him. But with a chance to relax and the chaos of the high-risk pregnancy, birth, and hospital stay now a closed chapter of my story, I was able to focus on myself. That's when I really started to notice it.

Thump. One, one thousand. *Thump.* Two, one thousand.

With each beat, my heart felt like someone pounding on my chest from the inside. And each beat came slowly. My portable blood pressure cuff said that my heart was beating somewhere between 38 and 42 beats per minute. This was nearly half of the 60 to 100 beats that were usual for a woman's resting heart rate. You could put your fingers on my neck and feel for a pulse, then count nearly a full second in between each beat. It was unsettling to say the least.

I called my doctor, and she kindly explained that experiencing a slower heart rate postpartum was actually common. It didn't happen often, but it wasn't rare either. It was something that happens to some women, and it usually resolves on its own after a few weeks. But despite her comforting words, I was still unsettled.

Honestly, I was terrified. Fear has a way of magnifying situations. Have you ever noticed that? Especially those moments where we are already experiencing uncertainty or stress. In this situation, the fear kept whispering, *"Sure, your doctor says it is normal, but what if . . . ?"*

I just wanted to sleep, but the slow beats made it difficult. I could feel each one pound through my body, reminding me over and over that things weren't the way they should be. I would lie awake at night, fearful that my heart would just stop beating altogether, and I would cry about what that would mean for my husband and my children.

I remember yelling out to God one night, "Don't you see me in this moment? Haven't I trusted You with everyone that has come before? Haven't I given You praise through storms scarier than these?" But He seemed silent. With all of the moments when He had spoken so clearly before, He suddenly seemed so silent! I didn't just feel unanswered. I felt unheard.

And that is when I decided to pound on the sides of the box again.

"DON'T YOU CARE THAT I COULD BE DYING?!" I yelled out loud through heavy tears.

And suddenly, I remembered the boat that His friends were in when they yelled the same thing. The boat Jesus was in too . . .

When Love Declared Peace

In Mark 4, Scripture says,

> That day when evening came, [Jesus] said to his disciples, "Let us go over to the other side." Leaving the crowd behind, they took him along, just as he was, in the boat. There were also other boats with him. A furious squall came up, and the waves broke over the boat, so that it was nearly swamped. Jesus was in the stern, sleeping on a cushion. The disciples woke him and said to him, "Teacher, don't you care if we drown?"
>
> He got up, rebuked the wind and said to the waves, "Quiet! Be still!" Then the wind died down and it was completely calm.[15]

See, the winds raged and the waters thrashed and the boat beneath them began to give way, all while the Lord slept. But then, all of a sudden, His friends looked around and finally realized who was in the boat with them. Yes. *With* them, and they cried out, "Teacher, don't you care?"

And just as the boat and the storm were not surprises to God, my moment and circumstances were no surprises to Him either. As a matter of fact, Jesus was the One who suggested that He and His friends climb aboard the boat. Not because He wanted them to be afraid, but because He wanted to teach them how to trust Him in the midst of the storm, despite their fear.

He wanted to show them the power of realizing who you can call on and what He can do when the seas get a little unsteady.

So, Love stood up and declared, "Peace!" And the winds listened, and the waves listened, and Jesus calmed the storm. Because that is what He does. He calms storms.

Many times I have read this passage of Scripture and wondered how Jesus's friends could be so foolish. Did they not realize that Life and Hope were in the boat with them? That Jesus Himself was a passenger of the very same boat!

But I see now that I am just the same. A little girl, now grown, crying out for my Daddy to rescue me. Forgetting that He is in the boat with me. Yet we are all the same. Each of us with our moments and each with our storms, holding on to the boat breaking beneath our feet, yelling to our God, "Jesus! Don't You see me in this moment? Do You not care that at any moment I could be swept off this earth?"

But, friend, He didn't bring you this far to leave you. He didn't walk with you through all of your previous moments of uncertainty only to abandon you when the seas get rough. He stands up and commands the waves and the winds, and they listen.

Because He is Jesus. And He speaks to hearts like He speaks to hurricanes, and He speaks to worries like He speaks to winds. With a word—with just one word. Because when Love declares, "Peace," even the most fear-filled waves cease. When Love declares, "Enough," even the most hopeless situations find faith.

Friend, hear me. Sometimes we pray for a miracle. We pray to be delivered from a season or a situation. And while God is able to do all things, often our rescue doesn't look like getting off the boat. It looks like being pulled from the fear and finding peace despite the storm.

Because even if the boat gives way, even if everything that keeps us feeling safe suddenly breaks beneath us, we don't have to fear the waves, because it was never the boat that kept us from drowning. It was never the security of where we placed our feet that kept us from being swallowed by the deep waters.

It was Jesus. And, friend, not only is Jesus in the boat, He walks on water too.

Are you in a season where everything that feels secure seems to be giving way around you? Sometimes a sudden change in our circumstances makes us feel unsteady. Sometimes an unexpected shift in our finances, our health or the health of someone we love, or our marriage relationship causes us to feel like we're going overboard. But, friend, you're safe.

Jesus wants to pierce the walls that contain your fear and flood every shadowed corner of your heart with hope. He wants to reach you in your sorrow and pull you out to joy. He wants to reach you in your fear and pull you out into hope. And above all, He wants to reach you in this moment, and pull you into His arms. Because what happens when we begin to see that the Lord is the lord over all? When we stop being afraid of the wind and the waves, we can keep moving forward in the storm, knowing that we will make it safely to the other side.

It took another month for my heartbeat to return to normal, and it took time to adjust to being a mom of three. But I wasn't scared anymore. Because I remembered that God wasn't surprised by the storm. He hadn't abandoned me in it, and as long as I listened for His voice, I would hear Him declaring peace and silencing every fear.

❦ Let's Talk

Scripture tells a story in Matthew 14 about a large group of people listening to Jesus around mealtime. Jesus's friends tell Him to send the people away so that they can eat. Instead, Jesus takes the food they have—five loaves of bread and two fish—and miraculously multiplies them so that there is enough to feed the entire crowd of more than five thousand people, with food left over.

One chapter later in Matthew 15, Jesus and His friends find themselves in a similar situation. A large group has gathered, and the disciples ask Jesus, "Where could we get enough bread in this remote place to feed such a crowd?"[16] Jesus takes the bread and fish that they have and does it again. This time He miraculously feeds over four thousand.

But I cannot help but wonder why Jesus's friends (who had just seen Him feed an even bigger crowd) would question how this need could be met.

Why wouldn't they just say, "Hey, Jesus, remember that thing You did a few days ago when You fed that big crowd? Do You think You could do that again? Look, we have some bread. We have some fish. That's all we needed last time."

Did they really forget so quickly? He had just fed a bigger crowd. He had just met a bigger need, and yet they don't seem to think that Jesus has any plans of intervening this time.

I think we do the same thing sometimes.

We find ourselves in need and wonder how Jesus could possibly come through for us. Forgetting all of the moments He has worked in our lives in the past.

So, friend, what storms are you facing right now? Are you being tossed about, trying your best to hold on while life seems to throw everything it has at you? Do you feel like you're going to be swept away in the current of chaos and drown in your to-do list? Do you have an urgent need in your health? finances? marriage? Does it seem absolutely impossible that the need can be met? Sometimes we find the faith that we need to face today's challenges as we remind ourselves of what God has already done for us. Take a minute to write out a few of the times that God has come through for you. As you do, I believe that your faith will be strengthened and you will remember that if God did it before, He can absolutely do it again.

_____

_____

_____

᪥ Let's Pray

Father God, thank You for listening to the prayers that our hearts have yet to pray. Your Word says, "Before they call I will answer; while they are still speaking I will hear."[17] You hear us

as we call to You. You see us in our storms. Father, bring peace.
Comfort our hearts. Strengthen our spirits, and send Your Holy
Spirit to bring hope to our souls. In Jesus's name we pray, amen.

Let's Hope

It won't always be like this. In a moment, God can change everything. He has done it before, and He will do it again.

9

The Father's Love for a Momma's Heart

GOD LOVES YOU JUST AS YOU ARE

There is an orange leopard-print chair in my living room. It keeps company with bluish-gray couches, and when people come over, it is often the first seat chosen. I always wonder why. It's not particularly comfortable, but it is unique; and for some reason, it is also apparently inviting. Over the last few years, many friends of mine have sat in that chair and shared their hearts.

Dreams have been given life, doubts have been put to rest, and many of life's issues have been wrestled with from that chair. I guess there is just something about having a place for a friend to feel safe to say the words that weigh heaviest on her heart.

But over the last few years, no matter what has been shared with me by the women who sit in that chair, I have learned that what many of my friends need to hear the most is simple: "God loves you, you know."

I am sure that these women have heard it a million times. I am sure that from the time they were very young, they have been told countless times of the Father's love. It is one of the first things we learn about God. Every Sunday school teacher and pastor and those sweet old ladies in church have said those words for decades to whomever crosses their paths.

But there is something about realizing the Truth behind those words. There is something about finally believing them. There is something about sitting down face to face with a friend you trust and having her look you in the eye and say them right to your heart.

So, friend, I need to tell you . . . God loves you.

Do you know that? You have likely heard that hundreds of times. It is likely those words are not new to you. But today, I want to ask you, Do you believe them? Do you know they are true? Because they are.

The very same God who formed galaxies and raised the dead to life knows your name and thinks about you. He does. He thinks about how you feel and the deep desires of your heart. He longs to have a relationship with you where you trust Him fully and believe that you are accepted by Him.

Do you know there is nothing that you could do to lose God's love? Nothing. Because there was nothing that you could do to earn it. He loves you because He is love and you are His. God loving you never had anything to do with you. It has always had everything to do with Him.

I know that sometimes the relationships in our lives (husbands, parents, other family members, and friends) all leave us feeling as though love is something we work for. We believe that love is something we earn by investing first. We think we must love to receive love . . . or something like that.

But too often, our relationships with others are broken at some level. It's an imperfect mirror of the Father's love, but often it is the only one that we have. So, with no other comparison, we believe that if this is what love is like, then God's love for us must be something similar.

But I need to remind you of something in the next few pages. I need to remind your heart that Scripture says that Christ first loved us . . . not because of anything that we do or don't do.[18] Not because of anything that we are or aren't. Not because of what we say, think, feel, or believe. He loves us because of who He is. Period. End of story.

Sometimes all it takes is for someone to remind us.

God loves you, friend, and when you believe it . . . well, that's when everything changes.

Desperate for the Father's Love

I had a friend in high school whose father was terribly mean. I had never met a harsher man than he. As a matter of fact, I would plan my visits to spend time at her house around whether or not her dad would be home. I was always afraid to be at her house when he got off work because I never felt very big when he was around. I never felt like I was worth much to him, and my friend felt the same way. There was nothing that she could do right. If her hair was up, he asked why she didn't have it down. If she was wearing a dress, he asked why she was trying to be so fancy. If she had her room clean when he got home, he asked why she hadn't washed the dishes too. And he was never kind in his comments about her personal appearance.

We never talked about it, but I often thought about how my friend must have felt. I could tell that she very much wanted him to tell her that he was proud of her, that he loved her. But the more she tried to earn his love, with no affirmation in return, the more exhausted she became. She continually sought his approval, hoping for some small sign. Until one day, when she decided that it was pointless.

She realized that it was impossible to earn his love.

She decided that she would look for approval elsewhere, and she found it (and lost it) in a long line of boyfriends that followed, never feeling fully accepted for who she was.

And so she sadly learned about twisted love, and how if you want to be loved in the world, you must earn it.

So much of what we believe about the love of our heavenly Father we learn from the men we call Dad here on earth. If we have fathers who are quiet, we believe God doesn't speak often. If we have fathers who are absent, we often believe God is uninterested in us. And if we have fathers who don't keep their word, are harsh with their words, or who say unkind words, we believe God is the same way.

I think this is one of the reasons we are so desperate for our children to have a father who is loving. We understand the importance of having a father who is gentle and kind and patient and how that shapes our children—and we often put this expectation on our husbands, hoping that they realize the great responsibility that rests on their shoulders.

But friend, just like you are concerned with the type of father your husband is to your children, I want to remind you about the truth of who your heavenly Father is to you.

He didn't wake up today and decide that you were good enough to care about. He doesn't think about that really awful thing you did when He decides whether He will love you anymore. God loves you unconditionally, but the last thing that the Enemy wants is for you to believe it.

See, the Enemy wants you to live like my friend. He wants you to feel small in the eyes of your heavenly Father. He wants you to believe that God doesn't think much about you at all. But the truth is, God delights in your presence. He adores you for you. But if the Enemy can convince you that you need to work at it—if the Enemy can convince you that every day is another day in a seemingly endless attempt to earn God's love and never feeling like you quite measure up—then he can distract you from the truth. He can distract you from the realization that it was not ever about your performance. God's love for you has always been based on your position.

You Can't Earn Love

Do you remember the first time that you laid eyes on that sweet baby of yours? Do you remember when the doctor or adoption worker or midwife introduced you to that new little life and you met for the very first time?

The morning Kolton was born changed my life. It had been a long night of labor and months of anticipating the moment that he would finally be safe in our arms. I had my chin to my chest and was counting out long pushes with the doctor and nurses each time the monitor indicated that I was having a contraction.

"One, Two, Three, Four, Five, Six, Seven, Eight, Nine, Ten!"

I exhaled, exhausted. I was sweaty and tired, and the only thing that kept me going, despite the many sleepless hours, was the thought of meeting my son face to face. I lay back against the pillow and looked up at the ceiling tiles. I closed my eyes, and then all of a sudden, the nurse said, "Okay, here's another contraction. This is going to be the one! Are you ready to meet your son? Breathe in and hold it! Now PUSH! One. Don't Quit! Two. That's it! Three. Here he comes!"

And the next thing I knew, brand-new life was lying on my chest, and I felt as if my heart would burst with love when I realized that this was my baby and I was his momma.

In that moment, there was nothing that Kolton had to do to earn my love. I loved him simply because he was my son. Kolton will never stop being my son, and my love for him will never be based on anything other than who he is to me. He can be mad or hurt or angry or sad, but he can never stop being my son, and I will never stop being his momma.

That is exactly how our heavenly Father feels about us. He loves us because of who we are to Him. We are His creation, made in His image, and when He looks at us, He sees Himself. He sees His children. And friend? That will never change, no matter what else we might try to believe.

ALWAYS AND FOREVER

Kolton has grown a lot, and now my nearly six-year-old wears all of his emotions on his sleeve. If he is mad, he says, "I'm feeling kind of angry, Mom." If he's sad, he cries. If he is happy, he opens his mouth really wide and claps or dances or does a really cool superhero move. I always know exactly how he is feeling.

One evening, as we were getting ready for bed, my son asked if we could read a second book. When I told him that we only had time for one book, he told me he was angry with me.

"I'm so mad at you, Momma. I'm not going to be your little boy anymore."

Now, honestly, I had to keep myself from laughing. Not because of what he said, but because of how he said it. I am sure that he was convinced in that moment that it was completely true. At such a young age he wasn't sure what not being my little boy meant, but in his eyes there was no greater threat.

"I love you, baby, and I'm sorry that you're angry with me," I told him, but I went on to explain that there weren't going to be any extra books read. As I left the room to go check on his sister, my son buried his face in his pillow. When I came back into the room, he was still there—crying.

"Kolton, what is it, baby? I'm sorry that we're not reading another story, but you're going to have to be okay about this. Let's just calm down and go to bed."

It was difficult to hear him because his face was pressed down into his pillow. Through big sobs into soaked sheets, he said, "I'm scared I'm not your little boy anymore."

He was afraid that his words had changed something that night. He was afraid that he had removed himself from who he was to me.

So, I picked him up, held him close, and reminded him again that there was nothing that he could ever do . . . ever . . . that would change the truth that I am his momma and he is my son.

But we do the same thing, don't we?

He Died for All of Us

Something happened—maybe a long time ago, maybe recently—but every time you get close to the Father, it holds you back. Maybe it is something you regret. Maybe it is something you haven't told anyone. Maybe it is something that you believe is unforgivable, but it tells you that maybe your relationship with your heavenly Father has changed. It has convinced you that you're not really worthy to go near Him. And perhaps you believe at some level that maybe He doesn't even really want you near Him because of that shame or regret.

But God's love for us was sealed when His Son died on the

cross for us. Jesus was the perfect sacrifice, and a once-and-for-all bridge linking the Father to His creation. Obligation didn't drive Jesus to the cross. Love was His only motivation. He knew that it was impossible to have a relationship with us without His sacrifice, and He knew that we were worth it . . . All of us were worth it. You. Me. Each of us.

Not just the good ones. Not just the ones who follow all of His commands. He died for those who will turn their backs and never acknowledge Him, just as He died for those who will spend their entire lives in devotion to Him. Because the love that motivated His sacrifice was never the love that came from us, it was the love from within Him. Jesus died for us because He is good and because we never could be.

And that same love has continued each day after His sacrifice was made. He loves you, friend, because of who you are to Him and who He is . . . never, never, never because of what you have or haven't done.

So, not only does the Enemy try to convince us that God doesn't love us, but he also tries to convince us that we don't belong in the presence of the Father at all. He tells us how worthless we are. He tells us how much we have done wrong. He tries to convince us that we are letting everyone down and that we are failures.

And eventually, if we hear something often enough, we just might start to believe it.

PJ Princess

Once, when my daughter was two years old, she came running into the living room. It was bedtime, and she was giving her daddy one last hug before bed. He scooped her up into his lap, kissed her on the head, and said, "I love you. Goodnight, princess."

I'll never forget her puzzled face as she looked down at her pajamas and said, "I not a princess. I don't have a dress."

You see, everything she knew about princesses included fancy dresses, and without one, she believed that she didn't deserve the title. My daughter looked down and believed that her position was based on what she wore, but as my husband explained, "You are my princess because you are mine."

Our Enemy wants us to believe as my daughter did. He tries to cover up who we really are by getting us to focus on what we lack. So he taunts us: *Just look at you. Why would you think that you're worthy of the Father's love? Don't you know what you've done? You're a bad mom. You're a bad wife. You're a failure at everything.* And we look down and we see shame, regret, and failure, all while forgetting that our relationship with the Father cannot be changed by what we have done, nor can it be covered by the lies that the Enemy wants us to believe about ourselves. We are daughters of the King, loved by the Most High God, and sealed with His love forever.

So, why does our Enemy care so much? Why does he make such an effort to get us to believe his lies? Basically, he is terrified that we might actually realize that we belong in the presence of God. We might actually remember our true identities as heirs to heaven. And if we do, then we might spend time seeking our Father's face.

Backyard Mowing

One of my son's favorite things to do is spend time with his daddy. If my husband is working on his truck, or in the yard, or simply working around the house, my son is right there with him. He watches his daddy. He learns from his daddy. He wants to be just like his daddy.

One afternoon three years ago, my husband was outside mowing. My son had been playing on the back porch, and I had been keeping an eye on him to make sure that he wasn't going to run out into the yard while Jared was still pushing the mower.

Jared was making the final passes on the edges of our property when I heard the mower shut off.

"Daddy!" My son shouted and leaped off of the porch, pushing his own little bubble mower. He lined his mower up behind his daddy's and waited for his daddy to start his up again.

I poured my husband a glass of water and walked it out to

him. He took a long drink, and my son reached up. "I want a drink too, Daddy!" Jared took one last sip, then handed the glass to our little boy. My son took a sip, then handed it back to me.

"Here you go, Momma. I'm gonna mow too."

My husband pulled back on the cord to start the mower, and my son pretended to do the same. Jared started walking, and my son followed right behind. For the next ten minutes, my son took every step that my husband took and followed him back and forth across our yard.

We are not all that different. As children of God, we have unlimited access through Jesus to the throne of God. We are welcome in the presence of the King of the universe! And not only does He simply allow us to come before Him, He also delights in our presence. Because God knows what we have learned as parents: the more time that we spend with our children, the more they act like we do.

The more time that we spend reading the Word or in prayer seeking the Father's face, the more we will become familiar with who He is, and the more we will naturally begin to act and speak and think like Him.

As Christians, we are called to act like Christ. We are called to be witnesses to the character and salvation of Jesus. But if the Enemy can tell us that we don't belong in God's presence—if he can keep us distracted or burdened, feeling as if we are not worthy of love—then he can succeed in keeping us from becoming more like Jesus. Jesus said, "Very truly I tell you, the Son can do nothing by himself; he can do only what he sees his Father doing, because whatever the Father does the Son also does. For the Father loves the Son and shows him all he does."[19]

Your heavenly Father loves you too. Sure, we've heard it a million times before, but when we truly believe it? When we remember that the Father's love for us is like His love for His Son? Then we win.

❧ Let's Talk

My dad has this story that he tells every chance he gets about a time when my sister was very little and he took her on a walk. He was carrying her when a large dog came out of nowhere and barked. My dad beams with pride as he describes how my sister responded. She didn't cry. She didn't cower. Instead, she looked at that dog and said, "My daddy!" as if to threaten it.

She knew that she was safe with her dad. She knew that he wasn't going to let anything happen to her, and she was right. It is a story that I love about my daddy's love for me (even though I wasn't the child that he was protecting) because my dad loved us both the same, and this story speaks of how my sister and I could trust him.

You know, Scripture tells us all about our heavenly Father's love. It tells us about how He healed and restored and had compassion on people. It tells about how He sent His Son, and Jesus brought with Him peace and salvation. The Bible is full of moments where Jesus proved His love for people; but sometimes we forget that if He loved them, then He loves us the same. Just as my dad's story with my sister told of his love for me, Scripture shows us all of the ways that God is a loving, trustworthy Father to us too.

What was your daddy like? Did you know him? I want you to spend a few minutes writing out who your dad was to you and about your relationship with him.

_____

_____

_____

Now, I want to ask you this: Do you feel that your dad was a good example of Christlike love? Do you feel that your husband is a good example? How can we tell the difference if we don't know God's character? The best way to learn about the character of Christ is to read stories in Scripture written by His closest friends. What are your favorite stories from the Gospels? From these passages, what do you learn about Jesus and what He thinks of *you*?

_____

_____

_____

❧ Let's Pray

Father, I thank You for being a good daddy. You're not just a distant father, but a daddy whom we are called to know personally. Thank You for calling us out of darkness and into the light. Thank You for pulling us out of the shadows of false condemnation and for speaking hope and Truth and life into our hearts. We decide this day that we will not let the lies of the Enemy distort our view of who You are, or who You have called us to be. Today, we will choose to remember that we are loved by God. You are not angry. You are not upset. You are not disturbed by our problems but delight in our presence. Help us to hear Your voice of Truth calling us to You. In Jesus's name we pray, amen.

❧ Let's Hope

I am loved. I am accepted. I am a child of God. Nothing I do can change His love for me.

10

The "Good Mom" Movement

YOU ARE ENOUGH

*W*e're coming to the end of these chats together, and I've saved one of the most important things to discuss until the very last. I know, we've covered everything from feeling all alone to feeling overwhelmed, and we've gotten to the heart of some really important matters in just a few, short chapters. But this is the part of our journey where I feel like I need to be as honest as I can, and I just cannot let you go until I'm sure this simple yet hard-to-believe truth is tucked safely in your heart. So, are you ready? Okay. Here it goes.

You are a good mom.

You skimmed by that too quickly. Read it again, would you? Here. I'll say it again. YOU are a good mom.

Has anyone told you that in a while? Or ever? Has anyone

looked you squarely in the eyes and told you that you are doing a great job? Has anyone held your hand and reminded your heart that this whole being a momma thing is hard, and it's normal for it to feel impossible some days? Has anyone ever admitted to you that she feels like a huge failure some days too?

Can I? Would you let me whisper a few truths into this place where our hearts are worn thin? Where the hours of taking care of little ones and juggling our to-do lists have all rubbed raw a place within us that never seems to fully heal? Where the ache of feeling like an inadequate momma just never seems to go away?

I need to tell you something, friend. Can I be real with you? Do you promise not to judge? I struggle with it too sometimes. No, really. There are days when something happens that causes me to wear the heavy shame of feeling like a terrible mom . . . all day long.

Sometimes it happens in the middle of the afternoon. The kids are fighting, and I'm trying to get the baby to nap, so I holler, "Go sit on your beds, and don't make a sound until I come get you!" And immediately, I feel guilty for how I have responded. I think about how they are just as important as the baby I'm rocking in my arms, and I wonder if they feel like I don't love them as much. I question why I couldn't just set the baby in his crib and give kind correction to my older children.

Why couldn't I show them love when they needed it the most? Isn't that what I would have wanted someone to do for me? Why did I have to shout?

Or sometimes, after a long day of feeling spread thin, I don't even consider my little girl's request to read another book. I don't even think about telling her yes, because I just want to fall into my own bed and sleep for the next seven days straight. And after the house is quiet, and the lights are off, I lie in my bed enjoying my five extra minutes to myself . . . all because I didn't read her another book. And then I feel so guilty.

I can't even enjoy my alone time, because I can't stop thinking about how I didn't spend as much time with my daughter as I could have earlier in the day. I wonder if she feels overlooked. I wonder if she feels loved. And so I get out of bed, and I creep across the house to peek at her. And suddenly I wish that I could wake her up and hold her close and tell her how much she means to her mommy.

Friend, there are days when I am sure that I've done it all wrong. When I'm convinced it's all my fault and that I'm a failure as a mother.

But I know that if I feel that way, then you probably feel that way too sometimes. Maybe it was something that happened when your child was little. Maybe it is a behavior that you cannot seem to change or don't know how to handle. Or perhaps the circumstances of your life have all aligned so that today, before picking up this book, you had the very thought, *I'm such a bad mom.*

Whenever that idea first crossed your mind, and whatever keeps it popping back up again, I'd like to speak a little heart-mending truth to you. And maybe I'll be speaking hope to my somewhat bruised mommy heart too.

So, if you'll let me, I'd like to remind both of us why we are not bad mommas. And hopefully, by the end of this thing, we'll have started a movement of women who want to speak truth into the hearts of other moms across the globe. Because when we mommas set our hearts on something, there's nothing that can stop us. And you and me? Well, together, we just might be able to change the world. But it has to start with us. First, we have to believe it for ourselves.

So, say it with me: "I am a good mom."

A Blistered Soul

Kolton was three days old, and I was already convinced that I was not cut out to be his momma. It was the middle of the afternoon, and I had decided to give him a little sponge bath (you know, because he still had that weird belly-button thing going on). I was careful not to get the water too hot. I was careful to not let him get too cold. I had a warm towel fresh from the dryer waiting to wrap him up as soon as I wiped him down. I had done everything right. But after he was towel dried, lotioned, and smelling like a delicious clean baby, I noticed that he had a small blister next to his right big toe—and I panicked.

(Side note: since that moment, I have learned that there are a few moments in motherhood that are worthy of panic. This was *not* one of them.)

"Mom! Come see this!" I shrieked from the nursery.

"What? What is it?" my mom asked, as she came running in from the living room, where she had been folding one of the first loads of baby laundry.

I held up a tiny foot for her to examine. "Kolton has a blister!" I declared dramatically.

She seemed less concerned than I thought appropriate for the moment. "What should I do?" I asked, still in a panic. Surely all her years of mothering had prepared her for such emergencies.

"Well, what do you want to do about it?" she asked me.

Now, you need to realize something. In my mind, at this point, I had two real options. I could drive him directly to the emergency room, or I could call the after-hours pediatrician. Fortunately for everyone involved, I decided to take the conservative route, and I went with the phone call.

Operator: "Thank you for calling the after-hours line.
  Can I get your name please?"
Me: [sobbing and barely understandable] "Yes. My son!
  He's got a blister!"
Operator: "Ma'am. Can I have the name of the child first,
  please?"
Me: [still crying] "Yes! My son's name is Kolton, and he
  needs help!"

It seemed like hours waiting for the pediatrician to call me back. I just sat there in the nursery crying and rocking Kolton (who happened to be sleeping right through our first big trauma together).

I was still crying when our pediatrician returned my call. Luckily, I wasn't the first new mom she had ever helped in her practice, and she knew exactly how to handle the situation — with grace. It turns out that Kolton simply had a place where the corner of his toenail had irritated his toe inside his little jammies. He and I both got some wonderful advice that day. I was instructed to put a little Neosporin on the blister and to take a long nap if possible.

To this day, I'm convinced that a long nap would solve a lot of mommy woes.

The blister incident taught me a lot about being a mom. I realized that a momma can go from completely sure of herself to a puddle of tears in as long as it takes to breathe in and out. I also learned that one small thing can cause her to question everything about her motherhood. I asked myself, *How long had that blister been there? Was it because his jammies were too tight? Was it my fault? How could I have missed it? Did I miss anything else? How would I ever know if I missed something if I didn't know I was missing it? Will I ever feel completely sure ever again?* I couldn't stop thinking about it, and no matter how many times someone told me otherwise, I was convinced that I was and forever would feel like a terrible mom. At least that was what the Enemy wanted me to believe. It's what he wants all of us mommas to believe. He wants us to live feeling like we are failures.

But I am not. And neither are you. But I want you to stop for just a second and think of times when you heard that lie.

We've talked about those old lies that the Enemy probably told Eve after she ate the apple in the garden. We've talked about how we hear some of them today. One lie that I'm sure was whispered thousands of years ago was this: *"You are a failure."*

It's a sneaky lie because it often sounds like our own thoughts. It sounds like something we came up with on our own: *I yelled again. I'm such a failure as a mom. The kids are both crying, and I'm so overwhelmed . . . I'm such a bad mom. All the other kids' moms are doing it this way, and I'm not . . .*

I wish I could just be a good mom too. We get stuck in a cycle of repeating lies to ourselves, convinced that they are truth. We try to remember all the moments that we did it right, only to have the Enemy whisper in our ears, *"But what about the time that . . . ,"* and we feel terrible, and we believe ourselves to be failures all over again.

This is one lie in particular that he taunts us with over and over again. Do you know why? Do you want to know why the Enemy wants us to live feeling like we are bad at everything we do? Because, friend, if we got a hold of the Truth that we are created in the image of God, that we are more than conquerors through Christ Jesus, that we are loved and called children of the most High God, we would be unstoppable. We could do anything. If we didn't live feeling like failures, there would be no limit to what we believed God could do through us and through our mothering . . . and the Enemy knows it.

He knows that our hearts would operate from a place of wholeness if we did not continually beat ourselves up over the things we do wrong. He knows that if we stopped feeling like bad moms, our self-esteem would improve, our marriages and relationships would flourish, and our mothering would take on a whole new confidence. Because our Enemy already knows what we have to learn for ourselves: when we are secure in who we are as women, and when we begin to find security in who we are as mothers, all other areas of our lives find healing as well.

So, we're going to say it together again, and this time, we're going to say it to put the Enemy in his place. Are you ready?

"I am a good mom."

That's It. They're Ruined.

I have burned many dinners in my day. As a matter of fact, the first few years of marriage, I don't think I made anything that would be considered completely edible. Now, don't get me wrong. We ate what I cooked (on the nights that I hadn't just ordered takeout), but that doesn't mean it wasn't burnt or black or didn't break a few teeth. Yes, I used cookbooks. I used timers. I even used thermometers to verify that the temperature on the gauge matched the actual temperature inside the oven. But despite having all the right tools and instructions, I couldn't seem to get it right. It took me a while to figure out how to be successful in the kitchen.

You know, when we first became mommas, there seemed to be a right way to do everything. From opinions of how to feed the baby, to where the baby should sleep and when, to dressing and diapering the baby, experts had an opinion on everything.

I wondered, *What if I screw up? What if I do something wrong and I mess up my kid forever?* It seems a little ridiculous, but deep down—almost six years later—I still worry about the same things. *What if I make the wrong choice and ruin my child?*

Just think about that word. *Ruin.*

That's tough. That's a heavy load. There's no coming back from "ruined." (I know, because I've seen ruined dinner.) But I think if we were honest with ourselves, the fear of making decisions that will harm the people our children will become someday is what motivates the majority of our parenting. We read the latest articles that tell us it is or isn't okay for our children to watch TV for X amount of time or play on iPhones or laptops—or even look at screens in general.

We follow the expert advice that helps us navigate the scary world of nutrition and everything related to GMOs and BPA and DHA. We correct our own parents who did *everything wrong,* like put us to sleep on our stomachs and let us eat food from the table at five months (and yet somehow we survived). But it is all motivated by that one underlying fear: *What if I make the wrong choice and I mess up my kid forever?*

If Only I Were a Better Mom

I want to ask you this: What would our parenting look like if we didn't operate in that fear?

I'm not talking about the commonsense concerns that keep our children safe. I'm talking about the fear that our own inadequacies will somehow hinder our children from becoming healthy and successful adults. The fear that we are somehow ill-equipped to successfully parent our children. The fear that we are bad moms, and bad moms raise bad kids who become bad adults.

What would life look like if we didn't believe that lie?

I think that one of the most unfortunate lies about motherhood that we believe is that if we were better mothers, we would have better children. Our kids would not act out as much, they would listen to us more, or they would do what we asked them to do without any fussing or fighting . . . if we were just better moms. But the truth is, when we look to our kids to find security in our parenting, we will only be left feeling disappointed. Not because they are a disappointment, but because their need for a perfect Savior does not indicate our failure as mothers. It simply means that they need Jesus just as much as we do.

The Confident Mom

The truth is, the fear of ruining our children will fade when we surrender our hearts to the Lord and say, "I cannot do this on my own. Help me be the parent that this child needs me to be." In that moment, we are not only acknowledging our dependence on Him but also our desire to be the best versions of ourselves for the betterment of everyone around us.

So, here's what I want you to do now, okay? I want you to think of the last time that you felt like a bad mom.

Are you thinking?

Okay, if you're like me, it didn't take you long to come up with something. I've got a couple ideas in mind myself that I need to deal with, so you're not doing this alone. Here's what I want you to do. I want you to imagine Jesus there in the room with you right now. Yes, right where you're sitting. I want you to invite Jesus to come and be present with you.

It can be as simple as a whispered, "Jesus."

Remember, He's not mad at you. He's not disappointed in you. He doesn't show up to make us feel like small, insignificant people. He doesn't show up to point out our faults. He comes to bring peace and healing and wholeness. That's what He wants to do for your achy mommy heart right now. He wants to take the brokenness and give you restoration. Friend, He wants to take away the mommy-guilt.

So, right now, I want you to take that moment when you felt sure you were a bad mom and were ruining your kids, and I want you to put it into the hands of Jesus. Yes, just hand it to Him.

There is no reason to hold on to it. There is no reason to keep it to yourself. Jesus already knows about that moment (or moments). There's no hiding it from Him, so there's no reason to try. He already sees it and sees you and loves you just the same. He doesn't want you to hang on to it like a punishment you feel you deserve. He wants your heart to be whole.

Remember, the Enemy wants you to keep it to yourself. He wants you to keep it secret so that he can keep beating you up about it. But, friend, Jesus came so that we might have life and have it abundantly.[20] He did not come so that we might have life and live it feeling like the world's worst momma. So, take that moment, and place it into the nail-scarred hands of Jesus.

Can you picture His hands? They tell the story of the sacrifice of love that He made for you and for me. There is a moment in an upper room where Jesus's friends are gathered and He appears to them after His death and resurrection. Thomas, who cannot believe his eyes, who simply cannot believe that Jesus (whom he saw die) is standing in the room with him, asks, "Can it really be You, Jesus?" And Jesus shows him the places where His hands were pierced by the nails that held Him to the cross. Thomas reaches out and feels the holes in Jesus's hands—and he believes.[21]

Friend, those same hands are reaching out for you right now. They already took the punishment for our sin. They already took the punishment for our shame. They already took the punishment for every area where we feel like we don't measure up. When we decide to live as though our shortcomings belong in our hands, we are choosing to ignore the sacrifice made by His hands. So, as you place your burdens and the moments where you felt like a failure in the capable hands of Jesus, I want you to see Him offer in exchange for them . . . grace.

What Would Jesus Say?

It can be hard to tune our hearts to the voice of heaven after we have listened to the Enemy remind us of our shortcomings for so long. What does Jesus even sound like when He speaks of our mothering? What would He even want to say to us? Well, one afternoon, I found out firsthand.

"You're a mean momma!" Kadence shouted, as I sat her down in time-out, then walked toward the kitchen. Her words hurt, but at that point, nothing she said could be worse than the words already playing over and over in my mind.

Why can't I get her to behave? A good mom would have this under control. A good mom would know just how to handle a strong-willed little girl both with tenderness and strength. A good mom wouldn't feel so overwhelmed. What if I'm ruining everything? What if how I handle this situation will forever change who she is as a person? Why can't I just figure this out?

It had been a long, stressful day. Nothing unusual had happened. It was just that our daily routine seemed a little bigger than all of us for some reason. I wanted to cry. I wanted to give up. But instead, I found myself doing something out of the ordinary.

I walked over and I picked up my sweet girl. She was a puddle of emotion and her tear-soaked cheek stuck to my shirt as she laid her head on my shoulder. She didn't want to act the way she had been acting. She just needed help. She needed to be reminded that she wasn't a bad girl—she was just having a bad moment.

With her head tucked under my chin, I began to remind her.

"Do you know that you're a good girl? You are so sweet and precious and smart. You do lots of things so well. You just had a few minutes where you made a few not-so-good choices. But do you know that I still love you? Do you know that there is nothing that you could do that would change my love for you?"

My words gave her a place to retreat. A haven of grace where her overwhelmed heart was safe from shame and embarrassment.

"Do you want to try again?" I asked, making contact with her three-year-old eyes.

And as she relaxed and peace washed over her, it was in that moment that I heard my heavenly Father saying those same things to me.

"Do you know that you're a good girl? You are so sweet and

precious and smart. You do lots of things so well. Do you know that I still love you? Do you know that nothing you could do would make Me love you any less? Do you want to try again?"

His words are full of grace for us, friend. His love for us is unending. He doesn't want you to live in shame and condemnation; rather, He wants you to live out of the overflow that He is enough.

We cannot care for little hearts on our own without letting Him love through us. We cannot expect to be good moms in our own strength. But when we allow ourselves to be washed in His simple whispers of grace, when we choose to hear the Lord say, *"We can do this together! I've got you, and I've got them, and I'm going to help you,"* that is the moment that we step out of the shadows. That is the moment where we stop feeling overwhelmed and start feeling like overcomers.

And that is when we begin to find joy in those tiny blooms of hope unfolding.

Let's Talk

I know that there are times when you're not confident in your choices. But maybe the healthiest thing for our children to experience is parents who might not be sure of their decisions, but who are sure of their Jesus. Who know that as they do the best they can, at the end of the day, they have to leave the rest up to the Lord.

Yes. We are going to make mistakes—but the Lord doesn't want us to be afraid of ruining our kids. He wants us to be motivated by love.

The Lord wants to be a part of our parenting, and I think more than anything He wants us to entrust our parenting to Him. He wants to guide us into healthy choices that are best for our families. He wants us to trust Him to lead us as we turn and lead our children.

How can you begin to let the Lord lead you in your mothering? What areas of your parenthood are you willing to surrender to Him?

As you consider the ways that you can find freedom in giving the burden of motherhood to Jesus, I want you to think of this. What would it look like if our generation of moms stopped living in insecurity? What would it look like if we accepted the truth that we don't have to be perfect to be the best moms to our kids? What would it look like if we started a movement of women who didn't focus on their failures but instead celebrated each success? You are a good mom, and it is not vanity to stand confidently in who God has created you to be.

So, I want to end our time together with a challenge. Now

that we are full of hope and surer of who we are in Jesus, I want us to consider our successes. No more focusing on the "mom fails," but instead, together we are going to change the conversation about motherhood. We are going to call ourselves good moms, and we are going to do everything in our power to remind all of the other moms we know that they are good moms too.

How can you encourage another mom this week? How can you get her to believe that she is a good mom too?

_____

_____

_____

❧ Let's Pray

Lord, we've had some negative stuff on repeat for a while now. We've been playing over and over in our minds all the ways that we feel like we have let down our kids. We have believed the lies that we just aren't cut out for all of this. But Lord, You knew just what You were doing when You made each of us moms. You knew everything that we would need to love our children the way they need to be loved, and You placed those things within us.

Lord, I don't think there is a mom out there who says to herself, *Today, I'm going to do an awful job. I'm going to make*

all the wrong choices. I'm going to mess these kids up for good.
No. We each do the very best that we can—every single day.
So, I ask that You would help my friend and me see that we are
doing a great job. I ask that You would bring peace to the places
within us that feel unworthy of Your love. I ask that You would
begin to heal the areas where we have been bruised by the lies
that we aren't ever going to be good mommies.

I ask that You would send the comfort of Your Holy Spirit
to fill my sweet friend with new life as she turns this page in her
story. May she point to this moment as the one where she began
to clearly hear Your Truth. May she go from here confident in
who she is in You. And may she fully believe that she is a good
mom. In Jesus's name we pray, amen.

Let's Hope

With God, I have everything that I need to be a good mom to
my kids. God is proud of me, and I am too.

Before We End

S o, friend, before our time together is over, I have to ask: Do you know Jesus? I mean, beyond just knowing *of* Him, do you know Him *personally*? Have you ever said, "Lord, I am not exactly sure what it means to give my life to You, but I'm ready to try"? Choosing to begin a relationship with Jesus is not complicated. It doesn't have to happen at a church. It doesn't have to happen in a group of people. We can simply quiet our hearts and have a short conversation with God. It might go a little something like this.

"God, I need You. I believe that I am broken and flawed. I am in need of a Savior. I owe a debt that I could never pay, but I believe that Jesus is Your Son. I believe that when He died on the cross, His blood somehow made a way and paid a price for me. I accept the sacrifice that Jesus made. I come before You, God, in the name of Jesus, ready to exchange my old life for a new one with You. Thank You, Lord. Amen."

If you just prayed that prayer for the first time, then *praise the Lord! I'm cheering for you! I'm seriously shouting and clapping and I couldn't be happier!* The next step is to connect with someone who is also a Christian. Call a friend, send an e-mail, reach out through social media, but get a hold of someone else who also knows Jesus and share your good news with them. They will be able to help you continue your walk from here! But I also want to hear from you and cheer with you! You can contact me at BeckyThompson.com. Thank you for allowing me to be part of your story. You are so very loved, friend!

Acknowledgments

As I think back on all of the steps that have led to this moment, I cannot help but thank and honor those who have walked this journey with me. This book has been possible because of their love and support.

To my sweet husband, Jared: Long ago, you told me that you would be first in line when my something special happened. You have always believed in my dreams with me. You have always done everything in your power to help make my hopes a reality. And you might think that this book is my something special. But, sweet husband of mine, you were first in line when my something special happened, because my first something special was you. I am so thankful for the gift of being your wife, and I am so grateful to have you as a partner as we walk through parenthood together. Thank you for every sacrifice that you have made so that I could passionately follow this calling. I love you.

To my beautiful children, Kolton, Kadence, and Jaxton: Someday, when you are old enough to read these words and understand them, you will see the hope that your stories have brought to the hearts of other mommas. You will see that your lives have revealed God's love not only to me but to others as well. Thank you for allowing me to share our moments. Thank you for reminding me of the goodness of the Lord daily. Thank you for the gift of being your momma. I love you so, so, so much.

To my momma, Susan Pitts: Thank you for being a good mom. Thank you for all of the love that you have poured into my life. Thank you for being the example that I could follow when I became a momma. And thank you for teaching me how to share the love of Jesus with others. I know how to tell about Jesus's love because of your stories and your ministry. Thank you for not only being my momma but my mentor in the faith as well. This book would not have been possible without you. You took a year off work, and you gave it to me—driving hours to come and watch my babies week after week while I completed this project. Thank you for every moment that you gave. We love you, Ninja Nana, and we are so thankful for you!

To my daddy, Marc Pitts: Thank you for being a good dad. Thank you for loving me like Jesus does. Thank you for not only telling me about Jesus, but thank you for also leading me to Him and teaching me what He sounds like when He speaks. Dad, I am sure of God's love for me, because of you. I am sure of God's goodness, because you taught me that I can trust Him. And it is because of your wisdom that I am able to share the Truth of the Word with others. Your legacy of faith lives on in each heart touched by the words written in this book. I love you, Dad.

To my in-laws, Steve and Kirsten Thompson: I am so thankful for the family that I gained when I married your son. You are such a blessing to our lives. Thank you for believing in us, and thank you for believing in me. Thank you for all the ways that you helped to make this book and this dream a reality. I love you both.

To my agent, Jessica Kirkland: Thank you for seeing the potential in me. Thank you for each moment that you spent encouraging me to find my story and for listening as I talked (and talked and talked) through my ideas. I am so grateful that you believed in me and were there to guide me. Thank you for connecting me with such a wonderful publishing house and finding such a great home for this book. I am forever grateful, friend.

To my phenomenal editor, Susan Tjaden: Thank you for recognizing hope before anyone else did. Thank you for taking a chance on me. Thank you for your wisdom and for your friendship. You gave me the freedom to write my story, while offering graceful guidance along the way. Your leadership made this process fun, and I am so thankful that we were able to complete this book together.

Notes

1. Philippians 1:6
2. Psalm 37:4
3. Daniel 3:17–18
4. Revelation 22:13
5. Psalm 37:23, KJV
6. John 4:7, 9–10
7. John 4:25–26
8. John 4:28–30
9. John 4:13–14
10. Galatians 5:22–23
11. Luke 10:38–42
12. Genesis 2:7
13. 1 Samuel 17:34–35
14. 1 Samuel 17:33, 38–40
15. Mark 4:35–39
16. Matthew 15:33
17. Isaiah 65:24
18. 1 John 4:19
19. John 5:19–20
20. John 10:10
21. John 20:24–29